STAND TALL LEADERSHIP

Stand Tall to Think Differently and Lead Successfully

Steven A. Bollar

JOSSEY-BASS™
A Wiley Brand

Jossey-Bass
A Wiley Imprint
111 River St, Hoboken, NJ 07030
www.josseybass.com

Jossey-Bass books and products are available through most bookstores. To contact Jossey-Bass directly, call our Customer Care Department within the US at 800-956-7739, outside the US at +1 317 572 3986, or fax +1 317 572 4002.

Wiley also publishes its books in a variety of electronic formats and by print-on-demand. Some material included with standard print versions of this book may not be included in e-books or in print-on-demand. If this book refers to media such as a CD or DVD that is not included in the version you purchased, you may download this material at http://booksupport.wiley.com. For more information about Wiley products, visit www.wiley.com.

Library of Congress Cataloging-in-Publication Data

Names: Bollar, Steven A., author.
Title: Stand tall leadership: stand tall to think differently and lead successfully / Steven A. Bollar.
Description: Hoboken, NJ: Jossey-Bass, 2020. | Includes index.
Identifiers: LCCN 2020022307 (print) | LCCN 2020022308 (ebook) | ISBN 9781119638896 (paperback) |
ISBN 9781119638964 (adobe pdf) | ISBN 9781119638919 (epub)
Subjects: LCSH: Educational leadership. | School management and organization.
Classification: LCC LB2806 .B586 2020 (print) | LCC LB2806 (ebook) | DDC 371.2—dc23
LC record available at https://lccn.loc.gov/2020022307
LC ebook record available at https://lccn.loc.gov/2020022308

Cover Design: Wiley
Cover Image: Courtesy of Steven A. Bollar

Printed in the United States of America

FIRST EDITION

SKY10075220_051424

CONTENTS

Introduction to Stand Tall Leadership

Obviously, Stand Tall Leadership has something to do with being tall, or not being tall enough, or a desire to be tall. What's the hook? There has to be more to it. If that is what you're thinking, you are kind of right. There is a connection to me being tall. Personally, I am 6′7″ tall. I have been this height since my first year in college. I was 6′6″ and then jumped one inch in college, lucky me. I look like I walked right off the college basketball courts into the NBA. Throughout most of my life, being a taller person was just something that I lived with. At times I loved it and at times I hated it. It isn't something that I could run away from. Just like you, your height is something that was given to you by your parents and ancestors. There isn't much you can do about it. But unlike most people my height started to truly define who I was as a person and ultimately as a leader within the schools.

Becoming a tall person wasn't something that I wanted. I fought the process as much as possible. Eighth grade was the year that everything went nuts. At the start of eight grade I was 5′8″. At the end of eight grade I was 6′3″. Basically, puberty kicked in and beat the hell out of me. I was constantly in pain. All of my joints hurt. I started having back pain. At night I would have muscle cramps so bad that I wasn't sure if I was going to be able to get up the next morning. Because I was growing so quickly and standing out from my friends, I started to slouch. I hunched my shoulders over and bent. I figured that if I did this I wouldn't stand out as much as I was.

One day during my eighth-grade year I was walking home from school with Danielle. Where I grew up, everybody walked home from school. Danielle and I kind of liked each other, so we would walk home together most days. I lived on Ninth Street and Danielle lived on Seventh Street. Once we turned onto Seventh Street, Danielle said, "Steve, stop."

I said, "Stop why?"

She said, "Just stop where you are."

I said, "Okay, why?"

She walked around behind me, and I was thinking, "What are you doing?"

She said, "Just stay still." She took one hand and put it on my shoulder. She took her other hand, balled it up into a fist, and punched me in the middle of my back.

I arched my back and yelled, "Girl, are you crazy?"

She said, "You are a tall person. Stop slouching and trying to be small – STAND TALL!"

At that moment it clicked. Everything changed in my entire world. I stood there and stared at her and I realized I wasn't being who I was supposed to be. Just to give you some perspective. . . my father is six foot six, my mother five foot nine, my brother is six foot six. I'm going to be tall! This is happening! Regardless if I was fighting it or not. When she punched me in the back, I realized I was not becoming who I was supposed to be.

I also realized that I was a leader. I was in student council, Boy Scouts, band, art club. I had leadership positions within them. People looked to me, they listened to me, and they observed the things that I did. I also realized that leaders are not supposed to blend in. Leaders are supposed to STAND TALL. Not necessarily physically tall, but within their actions and relationships. Standing Tall is all about your state of mind and how you operate within the world around you.

The start of my career was as a lower elementary visual arts teacher. Yes, kindergarten to third grade visual arts teacher. The little guys barely came up to my hip. I must admit, I did step on a few of them down there. They were just so small, and they move so quickly, it's hard not to step on a few and knock a couple down from time to time. I truly enjoyed being an art teacher. It was a dream job. Basically, every day I would host a party every 40 minutes throughout the day. Additionally, I was growing as an artist. My illustrations were being purchased and I even owned a mural painting business. As a visual arts teacher, I realized very quickly that my height was an amazement to the students and families. The students saw me as a giant. Most of the learning spaces within the school were designed for the little people. For me to maneuver and work within those spaces was difficult at times. In the beginning, the families were shocked that I was there. You don't often see a 6′7″ African American man teaching visual arts in a predominately white lower elementary school. Teaching at that school was a different learning experience for me on many levels. Eventually, I moved to the upper elementary school within the same district and then became the supervisor of visual and performing arts.

Most of my professional career was as a school principal. Fifteen years to be exact. There was some time as a curriculum supervisor, assistant superintendent, director, and superintendent. But the bulk of my time within the world of education was in the role as a principal. I must admit, I loved every second! There is nothing like heading your own building. The reason I became an administrator was because I didn't like administrators. I found them to be unimaginative, unwilling to take risks, uncollaborative, and just way too stiff. Usually you would think that if this is the norm for administrators, I'll just stay far away from it. Not me! My goal was to change what I saw in school administration. My goal as an administrator and specifically as a principal was to be creative, take smart risks, collaborate with others, and just loosen up.

As I moved through my career as a school principal, I continually made the connection between how I lived my life as a tall person and the leadership as a building principal. I was amazed at how the things that I did in order to adjust my life to fit within the world as a tall person and as a creative artist assisted me as a leader. Over many years I came to the understanding of what I now call Stand Tall Leadership. It is a blend of beliefs and lifestyles of tall people, the creativeness and risk of artists, and the practicality and strength of a school principal. Ultimately, it breaks down into nine areas that lead to the philosophy of Stand Tall Leadership:

- Stand Tall Leaders Should Not Blend In
- Stand Tall Leaders Have Influence
- Stand Tall Leaders Get Results
- Stand Tall Leaders Value Relationships

- Stand Tall Leaders Make Strategic, Smart, and Creative Decisions
- Stand Tall Leaders Take Action
- Stand Tall Leaders Use Their Voice
- Stand Tall Leaders Are Reflective
- Stand Tall Leaders Have Vision

Throughout this book we will explore each of these areas as it relates to the world of tall people and the role of being a school administrator, specifically a building principal. It will blend between developing strategies to improve, personal reflection, how to help others, and just have fun and be creative. Many of the areas of focus can be implemented into your life well beyond the role of principal and administrator in a school. Look at your life overall. See how it can help, improve, or maintain areas that you want to become better.

My motto is, "When you stand TALL you don't think small." This statement is the backbone of Stand Tall Leadership. A giraffe is the tallest land animal on the planet. The giraffe only knows how to see the world from the perspective that it has. It operates through the world confidently. It sees everything around. It has a level of vision and perspective that is unique. It knows so much more about the world that it lives in because of its perspective. The giraffe is unable to think like a gazelle. It does not have the lower level of vision like the gazelle. The giraffe operates at a much different level. The giraffe can see potential threats, food, and can answer the eternal tall question, "How's the weather up there?" This is true with Stand Tall Leaders. Once you see the world from a taller perspective . . . Once you see your role as a leader from a taller perspective . . . Once you experience your life from a taller perspective. You are unable to think small ever again . . . You now know what it is like. You know how to operate at a different level. Stand Tall Leadership will provide you that opportunity to see the world of school leadership at a new perspective. It doesn't matter if you are 4′3″ or 7′2″, you can Stand Tall as a leader and in your life. It's all a matter of perspective.

When you Stand TALL, you don't think small. #standtallstatement

Stand Tall Statements

Throughout the book I've added "Stand Tall Statements" that highlight some of the book's main themes, ideas, and takeaways. All of the Stand Tall Statements are Twitter-friendly and include the hashtag #standtallstatement. Please join me in the social media conversation about the Stand Tall Statement you found most helpful. Here's an example of a Stand Tall Statement.

Stand Tall Ideas

Here's the deal. As a school leader we are continually looking for new, fresh, and original ideas to improve our schools. We attend workshops and conferences with the hope of locating and finding a different way of doing what we do. Many times, we go to get training or go to a conference and we hear ideas that just reaffirm what it is that we already know, or the outcome of the idea isn't impactful enough to make the effort to do it. On the other hand, there are times that we hear amazing ideas, but we are unwilling to put forth the effort to actually do the idea properly so that we get the proper outcomes. Every now and then we get that one idea that is perfect! The ideas that we can easily or quickly implement into our leadership that will provide the outcomes that we are hoping for.

The opposite becomes true as well. We attend conferences and get a TON of amazing ideas that can be implemented quickly and effectively. We leave each training or session with pages and pages of notes. Each idea is better than the last idea. You are pumped up and excited about how your school and leadership will be transformed almost overnight. The people you meet and the conversations you have are rich with professionalism and pedagogy. There are others who think the same way you do, and you vow to stay in touch and keep the synergy going. Then when you get back to your school, reality kicks in. You put down your notebook and start working on the daily tasks that you usually do. You may do one or two follow-up emails with that other amazing leader you met, but eventually you lose touch. After about a month or two, you come across your notes and read them through. Your thought is, "Oh yeah, that was a good idea. It's too late now to start that."

This was what I experienced for years as an administrator. I would attend conferences continually searching for that one idea or get a ton of ideas and never do anything with it. I found my notes with tons and tons of ideas in them, but never did anything. I started to really think about what to do with them. I decided to take all of these ideas and turn them into a keynote, training, and workshop. I realized that educational leaders were looking for these ideas. They wanted to find that one idea that could work. Additionally, I started to figure out the best way to move from gathering a bunch of ideas in a notebook into real actionable items that can actually happen within my leadership. Therefore, throughout this book I will share a plethora of realistic and actionable ideas that can be easily implemented into your leadership and school to help improve the climate, culture, and relationships. By improving the climate, culture, and relationships throughout the school you will ultimately improve your leadership. Your level of influence will expand extensively.

Here's an example of a Stand Tall Idea.

Stand Tall Idea

High-Five Monday

At the entrance of the school, every Monday morning have a different group give high fives to students entering the building. Be sure to have music and bubbles as well. If you don't have different groups, you do it! The groups could be sports groups or clubs. Be sure to preassign the week they need to do it and have someone send a reminder out on the Friday before you start. It's a great way to kick off the week.

CHAPTER › ONE

Stand Tall Leaders Should Not Blend In

One thing that we all can agree on is that tall people don't blend in. When you look into a crowd of people, it is very easy to point out the tall people. Their heads seem to pop out from those around them. Usually, you see them bending down and back up again often. That is so they can talk and hear what is being said by all the "little" people around them. As a tall person, we are very aware that we do not blend in with those around us. We get that we need to make some alterations and changes to ourselves and surrounding in order to make our environment work. For example, the standard chair height is 18″, which is designed for people up to 6″1″. Therefore, anyone over 6′1″ needs to make some adjustments. Don't even get me started with airplane seats.

We also know that as a tall person we have a different view of the world from everyone else. What we see isn't what everyone else sees. Yes, that does give us an advantage. If we attend a concert, we rarely see the back of people's heads. It is a perfect view every time. When in a crowd of people if you ever need to get somewhere take your tall friend with you. He or she will be able to see the best way to get to the exit or restroom. It's like having GPS in a crowd. Having that level of vision and awareness is normal within the world of tall people.

When tall people speak, people listen. I think it's like a natural animal instinct. The bigger and taller the beast, the more authority it has. Therefore, others look to that bigger and taller beast and assume that the beast has something valuable to say or roar. I've found it rather peculiar how at times others ask my opinion on a topic or within a discussion that I have no part in. It happens more so when I'm standing than sitting. The physical presence and the desire to hear what the tall guy has to say is strong.

I truly believe that teachers and education are the last noble profession on earth. I also believe that every teacher, administrator, and support person within a school is a leader in some way. Whether you lead other adults or students within a classroom, you are perceived as a leader. The students and others within the school and community are watching what you do and watching what you don't do. The question becomes, what kind of leader will you show them? This chapter will focus on what makes a leader stand tall. A Stand Tall Leader doesn't blend in with others around them. You can pick them out of a crowd right away. A Stand Tall Leader has a different view of the world from everyone else. A Stand Tall Leader speaks, and others take notice. How does that happen? Even if the Stand Tall Leader is only 5′1″ with heels, it is all about how the Stand Tall Leader thinks, behaves, and acts on a daily basis.

Teachers and education are the last noble profession on earth.
#standtallstatement

Have you ever met a leader who was just like everyone else? If you did, I'm sure that the leader wasn't very successful as a leader. Who wants a leader who is the same as everyone else? If you do, you obviously don't want to grow as an organization. You are happy with just the way things are. What good is that? Yes, you want to have a leader who is relatable, understands your needs, and has similar interests, but just like everyone else? I don't think so.

1.1. Stand Tall Traits of a Good Leader

What makes a good leader? I ask this question when I give my Stand Tall Leadership seminars, speeches, or workshops. During the workshops, the participants have the opportunity to talk with their groups and report back what they believe what a good leader is. Over the many years of doing this, four distinct areas continually come up from educators that define leadership:

- Visionary
- Great communicator
- Makes difficult decisions
- Makes others better

Let's look at each one.

1.1.1. Visionary

Elena Aguilar wrote,

> A visionary leader is clear about what he or she believes and knows is best for children – for their academic, social, and emotional learning. The leader's individual beliefs have developed in collaboration with other stakeholders and articulated into some kind of vision or mission statement.

I find that statement to be true and nearly complete. Yes, a visionary educational leader is clear about belief and what is best for children, but according to the thousands of educators who I have trained, it is that and being able to develop an image or picture of what the school, district, or program could be and therefore able to share that vision with others so that they can all move forward toward that vision. Having a vision or mission statement means nothing if others don't believe in that vision. Others have to be able to see that vision. It has to become real and obtainable. As stated earlier, Stand

> **Having a vision or mission statement means nothing if others don't believe in that vision.**
> **#standtallstatement**

Tall Leaders are able to see things differently. They have a different perspective of the world from those around them. As much as that is a benefit of a visionary Stand Tall Leader, it does not carry much weight if the Stand Tall Leader is unable to share that vision with others. The goal is to have vision and share with others so that they can move forward together. If a leader is able to do that, does that leader blend in with everyone else or stand out and stand tall?

1.1.2. Great Communicator

There are so many books and articles about being a great communicator. We hear terms like *listen more and speak less, use less words, be clear, watch nonverbal communication,* and *be genuine.* All of them are correct. I am sure you could identify several more traits that make a good communicator. No matter what communication traits you list, it comes down to being able to clearly state what you want and getting others to do it or understand it.

Each organization has its own climate, culture, and history. That will determine what type of communication works best for the people within the organization. There may be a very open and cheerful climate and less formality is necessary when communicating, and the leader may be able to continually speak openly without worry of offense or misinterpretations. The climate may be very traditional and formal where all communication from the leader needs to be doublechecked and within the guidelines of policy and contracts. The organization may have a history of leaders who have communicated poorly so there is a lack of trust about what is being said. There might be a perception that there is a hidden agenda behind every statement. The ultimate goal of a Stand Tall Leader is understanding that no matter what type of environment the organization has, it must be able to clearly identify what the climate, culture, and history is like and then communicate in a way that would allow those within the organization to understand what the leader wants and be able to do it well.

A Stand Tall Leader takes the time necessary to think carefully about what is being said and the implications of what is said. There is nothing wrong with stating that you need time to think and respond appropriately. It is better to wait and speak with power than to rush and speak with uncertainty.

With that said, I ask: Is that a common trait of leadership? If someone is able to understand the climate, culture, and history of an organization and communicate in a way that gets people to act, does that person blend in with everyone else, or does he, she stand out and stand tall?

It is better to wait and speak with power than to rush and speak with uncertainty. #standtallstatement

1.1.3. Makes Difficult Decisions

There is a difference between making decisions and making difficult decisions. When educators were asked about traits of a leader, most of them stated that leaders make decisions. Then when I clarified and stated that leaders make difficult decisions, most would hum and nod their heads in agreement. Therefore, even though making decisions was the most popular statement, making difficult decisions was the most impactful statement.

Seriously, let's think about this. Everyone makes decisions. You have to decide if you are going to get out of bed every day. You have to decide if you are going to say good morning to someone else. You have to decide what to eat each day. Making decisions is too common an action to say about a leader. It truly comes down to making the difficult decisions that others do not want to make. Way back when I was a new administrator, I remember sitting in a meeting with a student, school counselor, and angry parent. They were all staring at me waiting for me to decide whether the student was going to be suspended. Mom had a scowl, the student looked afraid, and the school counselor had a look like, "Come on, man! You can do this!" At that moment, I realized the importance of making hard decisions as a leader.

Making hard decisions isn't easy, but someone has to do it. Some people tend to pull others into the issue so that they don't have to make the hard decisions alone and it's not all on them. Leaders don't always have the opportunity to do that. Yes, they might get the input from others to help them, but it usually rests on their shoulders. Later on, in the book I'll share with you specifically the five levels of decision-making. Not only do leaders have to make the hard decisions but they have to stick to them and make sure that others stick with their decisions. With that said, I ask again: Is that a common trait? Walk into difficult situations on a regular basis, make difficult decisions, and get others to follow those decisions. Does that person blend in with everyone else, or does he, she stand out and stand tall as a Leader?

> **Making hard decisions isn't easy, but someone has to do it.**
> **#standtallstatement**

1.1.4. Make Others Better

We would not be in education if we didn't want to improve the world around us. Specifically, making other people better than what they are. When educators talk about this in my workshops, they frame it as leaders helping those under them become better within their subject, with instruction, mentoring, and setting the example for others to follow. Basically, making others better through their own actions. Everyone within a school needs something different from the leader. Yes, even the 40-year veteran teacher who doesn't talk to anyone. A great leader understands the needs of those within the organization. Either individually, within groups, specific pockets, or as a whole.

Being able to gain that understanding and then acting on it is a skill that not many people have. The interesting thing about leaders trying to make others better is that leaders might think they are doing a great job but are failing miserably. I am sure you have either experienced moments or know situations where the organization is failing miserably but the leader is trucking along completely unaware, thinking that everything is growing by leaps and bounds. That level of being completely unaware isn't leadership. It is the inability to self-assess and make personal changes to ensure that the growth of others is taking place in the right directions. The most successful leaders are able to self-assess and properly connect their actions to the needs of others so that each person grows. With that said, I ask: Is that a common trait? Does that person blend in with everyone else, or does he, she stand out and stand tall?

The most successful leaders are able to self-assess and properly connect their actions to the needs of others so that each person grows. #standtallstatement

Think about the leaders that you admire. It doesn't matter if you know them or not. Do they Stand Tall?

- Do they have a vision and are they able to share that vision with others in order to move people toward success?
- Are they a great communicator by understanding the culture of an organization and molding their messages so that it is clearly understood?
- Do they step up and make the hard decisions when it is time and stand by those decisions?
- Are they making others better through continual self-assessment and personalized connections?

Think about yourself as a leader. Do you blend in with every other person in your organization? If the answer is yes, take a moment and think about how you are implementing the above into your leadership. If you noticed, none of them have to do with how tall you are. They do have everything to do with how you Stand Tall. Are you a Stand Tall Leader?

Stand Tall Action

Question people within your organization about what your vision is. If they are unable to explain it, adjust your communication style so that everyone knows it.

1.2. Hide and Seek

Tall people can't play hide and seek very well. There is just something about that game that doesn't work for us. Unless there is a tree or column around, we just can't seem to find a hiding spot. The only good thing about the game, depending on how you play it, is once found, we can usually outrun, reach, or tag the person who found them in order to not be "it." But to be honest, I rather be "it" anyway. If I'm "it," I don't have to worry about finding a place to hide. It is just too much pressure. Many times, when I would play hide and seek, I would purposely get found. "Oh darn, you found me. . . what a shame. . . I guess I'm it now. . ."

Tall people are always seen. They don't blend in with those around them. As much as I think that I don't stand out, I do. I am always on. Sure, I can walk around as if nobody can see me, but I know differently. The first thing they think when they see me is, "Wow, he is tall. I wonder if he plays basketball?" There are many times I don't want to be in the spotlight. I do want to play hide and don't seek. That time to hide and *don't* seek is valuable to me. It is time that I use to think, be alone, and make plans for what I want to do. Many shorter people take that opportunity for granted. It is common to blend in with the crowd and not stand out. Many people go out of their way to be noticed. But when your entire life revolves around people noticing you, blending in becomes something that you long for.

Many educational leaders have an open-door policy. Just to be clear, an open-door policy is the act of a leader literally or figuratively having your door open so that those under you can come in when they need to meet informally, share ideas, or discuss issues at any time. I remember interviewing for different administrative positions in the past, stating that I pride myself on having an open-door policy. Having an open-door policy is good in theory, but it lends itself to preventing you from getting any work done. Basically, you are a tall person on display all the time.

The thought of having an open-door policy is nice. You can imagine your staff coming into your office with a frown and after they talk with you, they leave with a smile. All of your staff loves you and you are the solver of many of their issues and problems. That may sound nice, but it just isn't reality. In truth, the staff come in at the moment you are trying to finish writing a difficult evaluation. They pop in when you are gathering your notes from a complicated parent meeting. They show up when you have to finalize your budget for the year before 3:00 p.m. and it's already 2:15 p.m. Each time someone comes into your "open door," you smile and offer an ear and your advice. How in the world can you get anything done? As a building principal, there were times I thought that if I heard, "You got a minute?" or "Are you busy?" one more time, I might just slap someone.

That does it! I'm shutting my door, and nobody can bother me. Slam!! After about 10 minutes of work. . . "knock, knock, knock." Who could that be? Can't they see my door is closed? You check to see, and it is Guilt standing there to reach out and give you a big bear hug.

The feeling of not being there for everyone can gnaw at you. Even though you are working alone in your office, you are hypersensitive to every sound, bump, or ring of the phone that is going on outside of your door. You feel guilty for not being there for everyone and for going back on your open-door policy statement.

What is administrator guilt? An administrator's feeling of missing out on actions and work that is taking place in the building or district and having remorse for focusing on one's self-growth or family, or for not handling situations within the school.

Examples of administrator guilt:

- Working on an evaluation and listening to a teacher scolding a student in the hallway
- Being a "manager" (of student and adult behaviors) and not an instructional leader
- Not attending every single event (concert, exhibit, sports, coffeehouse, etc.)
- Taking a sick day
- Taking a personal day
- Making the conscious choice to leave before your work for the day is done in order to be present for your family
- Being too exhausted from work to enjoy your own kiddos
- Having to ask staff to help cover for their peers who are absent
- Having to go to administration meetings instead of being on campus
- Being in data meetings instead of taking the data and going back to the classroom to help fix the data
- Not being able to give enough time to each teacher to provide adequate support
- Not dealing with a discipline issue in favor of an instructional leadership situation
- Missing amazing things going on in classrooms because I get stuck dealing with adults
- Not knowing all 582 student names on the spot and the names of their parents
- Taking a mental health day and not answering emails
- Not being everything to everyone

As a Stand Tall Leader, getting out of the spotlight is important. Similar to a tall person, as a leader you are always "ON." Even when you don't think you are, guess what? You are! Your staff, students, and community are watching everything you do. When you walk down the hallway, they are wondering where you are going. If you wear a new shirt, they are wondering where you got it and what it means. As a leader, you must be very aware that others are always expecting something from you. Therefore, you need the opportunity and time to get out of the spotlight and not be found. Work needs to get done. You are not wrong, and you should not feel guilty for closing your door.

1.3. Step It Up

When you take time to get out of the spotlight and close your door, the world will not come to an end. True, things may not go exactly the way you want it to, but you can be assured that it won't blow up and crumble to the ground. The goal is to train up those around you to be able to handle issues and concerns. When you are not there for every little thing, the staff builds problem-solving skills. What better way for your staff to become better at solving issues than to have issues to solve? They need to step up. It may take some time to get them to where you want them to be. You may need to go through the process of the levels of Stand Tall Decision Making (see page 92). By having those around you step up their game for decision making, you can be less guilty for shutting your door and taking time do what you need to do so that you are a better leader.

> **What better way for your staff to become better at solving issues than to have issues to solve?**
> **#standtallstatement**

1.4. Timing

When choosing to get out of the spotlight and get work done, it doesn't have to be sporadic. As a building principal, my assistant superintendent visited me to check in every month. One time when she was visiting, I was interrupted about four times in a row. She asked me if the interruptions were a problem. Trying to act like I could handle everything, I responded that it wasn't a problem and it was rare to have four interruptions in a row. Actually, it is usually about six to seven interruptions in a row. She suggested that I put time in my calendar to close the door and have uninterrupted time. I could read an article, reflect on my leadership, or plan the upcoming week. It doesn't matter what you do, you just need to schedule it or it won't happen. Schedule when your door is open and when it isn't. Live by your calendar and be committed to that time. Let your secretary know that time is sacred. Don't let other things get in the way of your time. Having my direct supervisor give me permission to take that time was huge. It allowed me to give guilt a big slap. So, if you need permission to take some personal time, I'm giving it to you now.

I know, I know, I know. . . at first you will do it for a week or two, and then you may start making excuses for not taking the time. After a month or so, your time is gone, and the pop-ins continue. You are back to what you were doing before. You need to resist the temptation to make excuses. Make sure everyone knows about this time for you to get away and hide. If you need to rotate the time so that you are not alienating the same people every day or week, that is fine. Just schedule the time and stick to it.

If you need permission to take some personal time, I'm giving it to you now. #standtallstatement

1.5. Practice? It's Just Practice!

When you have time to think things through and practice how you will respond, you come out as a better leader. You are a more polished, prepared, and stronger Stand Tall Leader. It is amazing how on television shows they always say the right thing all the time. Even if they are supposed to say the wrong thing, they say the wrong thing the right way. That is because it is fake, and the actors rehearse what was going to be said and how to say it. Imagine if you as a leader were able to say and do the right thing all the time. You were polished and prepared, especially when things around you were going crazy. That only happens when you properly prepare and rehearse prior to the actual event. When is that practice supposed to take place? Exactly! It usually doesn't.

I used to be so proud of how I could react on a moment's notice within my position. I thought that the outcomes I produced were best when I was pushed, and I operated on instinct. Boy, was I wrong about that. Within my second year as a principal, I had a faculty meeting after school. One of my teachers challenged me with a question about a building management process within the school. I quickly provided an answer and tried to continue with the meeting. Immediately afterward, she asked another question. I responded to that question as well. Then others asked another and another and another question. As a school leader, I am sure you have experienced this. Eventually, I had to stop everyone, stating that I would figure it out and get back with an answer. I wouldn't have minded playing hide and seek at that moment. The next day, I realized that I needed time for myself to think and prepare how I was going to solve the issue and respond appropriately.

Upon reflection and time, I was able to be better prepared and a stronger leader. Take the time you need to get out of the spotlight and reflect on being a leader. It is okay to do this. Others who work with you will be empowered and you will respond much better to those around you. You will be amazed at how refreshed you will feel after having the time to think and practice how to react and respond. Thinking is a valuable commodity that does not happen as often as you would hope. Most of the time as school leaders we are reactionary and on auto pilot. We even get comfortable with operating that way on a regular basis. The sad part is that when we do have time to think, we get FOMO (fear of missing out). When we are behind closed doors alone, thinking and practicing, we think that we are missing out on something that is happening in the school. It's hard to truly shift our thinking toward what we need to be thinking about. Even though we are in our own thoughts, we have an ear out to the noises in the hallway—especially if it is *too* quiet. It's like when you go on vacation. It takes a day or two to truly wind down and start to fully immerse yourself in the vacation experience. It takes practice for you to get used to having time to think and practice. Work with your office staff and other leaders to carve out time to make it happen. Put it on your calendar. Then keep that schedule. It will help you become a Stand Tall Leader.

When you have time to think things through and practice how you will respond, you come out as a better leader. #standtallstatement

Stand Tall Action

Look at your weekly calendar. Pick at least one date and time a week to go into your office, close the door, and do something to improve yourself as a Stand Tall Leader. Ask or tell someone else to help protect your time. Don't answer phones or email. This is your time to help you become a better leader. Make sure you place it on your calendar. Don't lie to yourself and not do it. Start with once a week and then move it up to at least two times a week.

Stand Tall Ideas

Out of the Office Day

One of the challenges for administrators is getting away from paperwork and being stuck in the office. Yes, it is important to get the office work done and there are deadlines that must be met. When administrators get out of the office, it is usually for an observation, walk through, or to solve an issue. Out-of-the-office day is a dedicated day to stay out of the office and to visit classrooms, students, and

(*Continued*)

staff for no reason but to visit. There is never a perfect day to do this, so just pick a day and go for it. It is important to notify your staff ahead of time that this is your official out-of-the-office day. Make sure they know you are around just to enjoy the school. No formal observation. No follow-up conversation. No responding to emails. Have the office secretary be aware to "hold down the fort." If you are fortunate and have other administrators on staff, have them cover for you for the day. Once you get over the anxiety of being away from the office, you will find it to be one of the most rewarding days of the year.

Pat on the Back

Have you ever had a moment in time when you said something or did something amazing, but nobody was around to see it? How about, you worked through a difficult problem with little to no help from anyone else? Better yet, have you ever accomplished a goal that you have set for yourself that nobody else knew you were shooting for?

If you said yes to any one of the above questions, you are not alone. Actually, you are alone! That is the problem. We all know how important it is to provide recognition to others when they do well. Who is there to recognize you when you have done something great? Often, you are alone. You would like to share with others your triumph, but you feel like you would be bragging or boasting about your accomplishment.

You need to make sure you take the time to give yourself a pat on the back. I printed the copy of my hand and placed it on the wall. Whenever I do a good job with something, I walk over to my hand on the wall, turn around facing away, and give myself a pat on the back. It only takes a few seconds to push my back against my hand and say good job to myself.

It is vitally important that you praise yourself when you do a good job. You are your best advocate. You can also be your worst critic. So often, people put themselves down and look at everything they cannot do. I am giving you permission to celebrate you! It is not vain. It is not cocky. It is not arrogant. It is personal time to motivate yourself and keep the fire alive.

Another option with this idea is to cut out small hands. Share the story of giving someone a pat on the back. Students can purchase a "Pat on the Back" hand as part of a school fundraiser. Write the name of the person who receives it on the back and have them delivered.

Stand Tall Ideas

Principal's Webpage

The focus of the principal's web page is to express your vision for the school and educational philosophy. Additionally, you want the school community to get to know you. Here are some suggestions:

- School mission statement: Hopefully, the mission is not a three-paragraph-long statement that nobody wants to read. As long as it is short and to the point, put it on the page. Also, a few sentences about how you believe in the mission would be beneficial.
- Test scores before you started and test scores now: Consider showcasing test scores that were not as good before you started as principal, and now how much better they are. You can add a few statements about how the staff works hard with the students to get great results. If the scores are not better or the same, I wouldn't suggest posting them.
- Basic demographics: Not the demographics of the school, demographics of you! If you are comfortable, share the town you are from, the number of kids you have, how long you have been married, years of experience. This information will allow the community to build a relationship with you. If they know you better, they will trust you more.
- Favorite quotes: People love positive quotes. Grab a few and post them on your principal's page. Consider a couple of powerful ones and toss in a funny one that everyone knows. Again, this will allow others to get to know you and will build trust.
- Favorite educational movies: I tried this one with my monthly newsletter, and I got a huge response from the parents. Some parents sent me emails and others shared how they rented the movies because of my suggestion. Try it and see what happens.
- Vision: Share where you see the school going within the next few years. Sharing the vision of the school pulls others into the vision and heart of the school. The more people connect to the vision, the more understanding they will be when decisions are made.
- Where is the principal? Have a section that is updated monthly that shares part of your schedule. Share that you will visit a community soccer game, PTA meeting, school board meeting, or go whitewater rafting on the weekend. It shows that you are a professional and normal person - another opportunity to build relationships and make connections.
- Photo: You need two photos: one serious and one having fun with kids. I strongly suggest you get them professionally done. Every school has a staff member who loves to take photos and has a great camera. Have that person take some good shots. Don't just have the typical school photo. You need to show some personality.
- Link to a great article: As you find great articles about education, post them to your website as a reference. Doing this shares your educational philosophy. Providing a writing of your thoughts on the article is icing on the cake. Not only are you well read, but well written.

(*Continued*)

Do *not* include on the website:

- The weather
- Why you made certain decisions
- Information about other schools
- Only data
- The same thing you had last year
- One looooooonnnnggg paragraph (nobody reads them)

CHAPTER › TWO

Stand Tall Leaders Have Influence

2.1. Influence

Visionary, great communicator, making difficult decisions, and making others better. If you put these four traits of a leader together, what is it that a leader is ultimately doing? Ultimately, the leader is having an influence on others. Influence is *the capacity to have an effect on the character, development, or behavior of someone or something.* Basically, isn't that what we want leaders to do?

People are going to be people. People have free will to do whatever they want to do. A leader's job is to influence others to operate in a way that improves themselves and the organization. A leader does that in multiple ways. One of the most popular ways it is done in education is through having a clear vision, being a great communicator, making difficult decisions, and ultimately making others better. When a leader's influence is strong enough, things start to change. People adjust their behavior to either fit or avoid that influence.

Let's be honest, there are some bad leaders out there. Even though they are bad, they still have influence. It's not good influence, but it is influencing nonetheless. The goal is to use the skills that make you stand out from others in a positive way and to guide others toward continual improvement.

Blending in isn't something that Stand Tall Leaders do. It doesn't matter if you're 4′11″ or 6′8″, you can Stand Tall as a leader. It's how you carry yourself. It's what you say. It's how others perceive you. It's the difficult decisions you make. It is the influence you have on others.

After my friend punched me in my back, I realized that I needed to change. I changed the way that I walked, thought, and how I interacted with other people. I carried myself with pride and started my journey toward learning as much as I could about leadership and how to have a positive influence on others. This is the basis of Stand Tall Leadership. . . Yes, I'm tall and it's very obvious you can't miss it. But being a Stand Tall Leader is about having the thoughts, concepts, and actions to influence others under your charge to move in a positive and productive direction. You are currently a leader or in the process of becoming a leader. When you stand TALL you don't think small.

Influence is the core of leadership.
#standtallstatement
Blending in isn't something that Stand Tall Leaders do.
#standtallstatement

Reduce, Not Eliminate

The concept of *reduce, not eliminate* relates to the reality of educational leadership, classroom management, student data, and a plethora of other important areas within education. The purpose of understanding *reduce, not eliminate* is to help educators operate within reality instead of operating with the false understanding of how things should be.

Reduce, not eliminate, is about the true expected outcomes that you want to take place. In almost all cases we look to eliminate the issue, problem, or behavior. We have meetings and dialog about how we can make it go away. We develop plans and action steps to eliminate the problems and have the positive productive outcomes that we want. The problem is that you may never eliminate anything. Complete eradication is impossible. No matter how many meetings you have, plans you develop, or strategies you implement, the concern will not be eliminated. You are setting yourself and others up for disappointment. Now that it has not been eliminated, we start to complain about how the idea or program "didn't work." This is why you don't get the buy-in that you wanted for the new strategy. Over time, educators have been exposed to program after program after program that does not eliminate the bad grades, behavior, or low-test scores. This is when you have educators saying, ". . .Here we go again." Stop saying you are going to eliminate and start saying reduce.

Instead of expecting the elimination of the problem, start expecting the reduction of the problem. By focusing on reducing instead of eliminating, you will have a more realistic understanding of how things could be instead of how things should be. People are people. No matter how much influence you have over them you cannot control everything to ensure the elimination of issues and problems. What you can do is use your level of influence to reduce the probability of issues and problems. I can live with a reduced probability. If the probability of problems and issues is reduced, then the probability of me doing what I want to do increases. Now I can make progress!

Reduce, not eliminate is not about being a cynic. You are not a downer who thinks that a solution will never take place. It's about being realistic about what can be accomplished and then celebrating that accomplishment. Embracing *reduce, not eliminate* is a relief. A huge burden should be released from your shoulders, knowing that you are working toward a goal that IS obtainable instead of a false reality that give you stress. Reduce, not eliminate, reduces administrator guilt, teacher guilt, and leadership guilt.

Examples of Reduce, Not Eliminate

- Poor student behavior
- Time off task
- Poor teacher behavior
- Poor instructional strategies
- Low parent involvement
- Opting out of testing
- Poor attendance
- Frequent lateness
- Teacher absenteeism
- Poor test scores

By focusing on reducing instead of eliminating, you will have a more realistic understanding of how things could be instead of how things should be.
#standtallstatement

2.2. Integrity

What is *integrity*? Personally, I think integrity is a set of beliefs, values, and actions that others can depend on. Everyone has integrity. Some people have high integrity and some people have low integrity. Either way, it is there. Those beliefs, values, and actions may have high moral standards, or they may be extremely low moral standards. Regardless of where the moral compass points, others know where you stand because you are consistent with your beliefs, values, and actions. Of course, everyone wants to have high integrity. The challenge comes when conflict arises. Conflict can bring out the best and the worst in people. In most cases, people are very reactionary when faced with a conflict. The true YOU comes out for everyone to see. In order for the true YOU to maintain a high level of integrity during conflict, you need to practice in times when there is no conflict.

You don't establish integrity immediately. Integrity is developed over time. Others need to experience your beliefs, values, and actions. They have to hear you say it, watch you do it, and watch you say and do it again. There needs to be a pattern of continual behavior that is consistent with what you say and believe. There are times that others have experienced your level of integrity and can vouch for you. That only goes so far. New people in your life need to experience your integrity firsthand.

For an example: Do you know someone who is always late? It doesn't matter what the situation is, you know this person is going to come in late. It is a belief, value, and action that you can depend on. Do you know someone who is always on time? It doesn't matter what the situation is, you know this person is going to be on time or early. Again, it is a belief, value, and action that you can depend on.

The important part is not only to establish your level of integrity but also to maintain that level of integrity.

2.2.1. How to Maintain a High Level of Integrity

2.2.1.1. Keep Your Promises

People remember promises. Promises have a heavier weight than other statements. A promise states; no matter what I will follow through with what I said. Promises are usually reserved for your big issues, projects, and events. When a promise is broken everyone takes notice. Yes, you can apologize, and they may accept the apology, but your actions are logged into the memory of others. At times, emergencies come up that prevent you from fulfilling your promise. You must do whatever you can to make up for the missed promise. Just letting it go isn't enough. When others see over time that you are keeping you promises, doesn't that help maintain a higher level of integrity?

2.2.1.2. Err on the Side of Fairness

When it is time to make a decision, always choose what is most fair to all involved. People are naturally selfish. We tend to look out for self. If you are the one making the decision, make sure the outcome is as fair as possible to everyone involved. Think back to times when you were not treated fairly by someone you knew. What did you think of his/her integrity? Even if that person continued to be fair after the one incident. Your view of that person's integrity was forever changed.

Fairness goes both ways. Are you the type of person who tends to take too much on their plate in order to always provide support? How is that fair to you. Over time, others will realize that they can "get over" on you and take advantage of your generosity. Remember, integrity is a set of beliefs, values, and actions that others can depend on. If others can depend on you always taking everything off of their plate and putting onto your plate, is that fair? There is nothing wrong with getting what's coming to you. Over time, people will know that what you are willing to do for them is fair because both of you are held equally responsible.

2.2.1.3. Speak Out for What You Believe In

If something is important to you, say so. Nobody respects a person who folds with the common perspective all the time. Your voice is important. If you agree with something, speak up and say why. If you disagree with something, speak up and say why. Either way your voice is heard, and others will respect you for that. Remember, as a Stand Tall Leader you don't blend in; everyone sees you anyway. They are waiting to hear what you have to say. If you say nothing, that says something too. As you know, there is a right way to speak out and a wrong way to speak out. Understand your environment, culture and climate and speak out appropriately to get your point across and be heard. The focus is that others will realize that you are genuine, passionate, and willing to look at all perspectives. Even if the perspective goes against the grain.

2.2.1.4. Do What You Say You Are Going to Do

This is very close to keeping your promises. This point focuses more on your daily actions and goals. If you say you are going to arrive to a meeting on time, do it! If you say you are going to finish the report, do it! If you say you are going to reflect on your day, do it! What you do throughout your day consists of many little decisions. As a Stand Tall Leader, others are watching what you do and what you don't do. They can see if you are one to keep your word with others and yourself. If you say it out loud or in your head, follow through and make it so. I would argue that doing what you say you are going to do is the most important part of developing and maintaining a high level of integrity. Not doing what you say you are going to do damages your integrity on a daily basis. Doing what you say you are going to do reinforces your integrity on a daily basis.

When I was a child, my family did not live near a shopping mall. Therefore, it was a big deal to have the time to go. My brother and I begged my father to go. Eventually, he said yes. He stated that he promise to take us in two weeks. During the two-week time, my brother and I saved our money from our paper route. Finally, the day came. We piled into the minivan and my father started the drive to the shopping mall. About five miles outside of town, my father started to scream in pain. He was holding his abdomen and pulled the car over. What was going on? This was before cell phones, and neither my brother nor I could drive. Eventually, my father was able to turn the minivan around and drive home. Once home, my mother took my father to the hospital. It turns out, he had several gallstones that had to be removed.

About two months later, my father came to my brother and I and said, "Let's go. I'll take you to the mall." We both explained that it was okay, and we didn't have to go. Not to mention, we had no money. My father stated that he made a promise and he was going to keep it. He reached into his pocket, gave us money, and took us to the mall.

Integrity is so much more than keeping a promise or two. It shows the world who you are. It identifies your character and level of respect for others and yourself.

Living with integrity means:

- ***Not settling for less than what you know you deserve in your relationships***
- ***Asking for what you want and need from others***
- ***Speaking your truth, even though it might create conflict or tension***
- ***Behaving in ways that are in harmony with your personal values***
- ***Making choices based on what you believe, and not what others believe***

– Barbara DeAngelis[1]

Integrity is a set of beliefs, values, and actions that others can depend on.
#standtallstatement

2.2.2. The Value of Integrity

Integrity is the cornerstone of your leadership. Integrity is the backbone of your character. Integrity is the substance of your legacy. Others will continually witness and experience what you believe, value, and act on, and from that, they will develop a deeply engrained opinion of you. That opinion will guide their level of commitment.

[1] Barbara DeAngelis, *Real Moments: Discover the Secret for True Happiness* (New York: Dell Publishing, 1994), p. 99.

As a Stand Tall Leader, do you want others to be committed to you? Do you want others to accept your influence? If you do, you must continually work to maintain a high level of integrity. Once you leave your position of leadership, your legacy will remain. What will that legacy look like? Your legacy will match your level of integrity. Maintaining a high level of integrity is an ongoing process that allows you to be a Stand Tall Leader.

2.3. Compliance vs. Commitment

There's going to be times that you will roll out new programs or help reinforce programs, directives, and necessary rule changes. One of the main things that many leaders always worry about is getting buy-in. How are we going to get buy-in from the teachers? How are we going to get them to join with us with this directive? How likely is this to happen? There are some things that you need to keep in mind and understand as it relates to getting buy-in or getting others to go along with what needs to be done. There's the difference between complying with whatever it is that's being done and committing to it.

Compliance means that there are rules, expectations, or policies that need to be followed. But following through with these requirements doesn't mean that you agree with them. It just means that this is my job, this is my contract and I have to meet expectations, so therefore I am doing it. Whenever anyone is complying with expectations, they are giving an effort. They are not giving their best effort. Just an effort. They are not giving 100 percent of their effort. Sometimes you have those that give 100 percent all the time. They do go above and beyond regardless if it's something they have to fit in compliance or not, but for the most part, many will comply with whatever information is given. If they disagree with it, there is a process. It may be internal struggle, they talk to others to get agreement that they do not agree, or they may go to the leader and complain. At times as leaders, we're content with compliance. Since they are complying, we had better just be quiet and live with what we got, at least got them to comply. That's good enough. To be honest, as much as compliance is good, it's not truly getting 100 percent to make programs, events, and ideas become exceptional. Compliance is a low level of accomplishment.

The way that we can move a program, an idea, and concept to the next level is through having commitment. When staff members have a commitment to our program idea or an expectation, they give so much more. The outcomes are so much stronger. When you have that commitment to finding the outcomes and getting what it is that needs to be done the results far outweigh expectations. Now the question comes in, how do you get people to have commitment beyond just basic compliance? The way that you get commitment to something beyond basic compliance is not through rules, outlines, data, and detailed expectations. It's through the heart. It's through inspiring them see the vision, allowing them to understand and feel their role in the bigger picture of things. Inspire them to see the benefit from what needs to be done? See how their students benefit? Sometimes that benefit isn't test scores. Remember, teachers don't necessarily care about test scores as much as leaders, administration, media, and everyone else.

Quality teachers think about making commitments with students and seeing that growth in many different ways. Ultimately, the only thing that teachers really want to do is teach. When they have that connection where they are committed to finding that growth and getting the best out of their students and those around them; that's when you see that amazing transformation take place. I am sure it is either the same or close to the vision you have for your building. There are certain things from a leader's perspective that need to be done in order to get that high level of commitment. Connecting with the heart, sharing stories and painting a picture of what the true outcomes could be. Showing staff how they benefit from the actions being done. Having them be able to express and say back to you how they feel and how they want to see this manifest itself. It also comes through many of your other actions and the level of integrity you have developed with them. There needs to be a history of positive beliefs, values, and actions that they can depend on over time. Living the vision on a daily basis strengthens the commitment from those you lead.

You want them to truly love it. You want them to be able to do well with it. With that being said, as the actions and the processes are done, many times your goal when you're developing that commitment from others is to simply be a cheerleader, be a guide. Cheer them on, reinforce the vision and help them be able to do what needs to be done. Compliance is great. It allows us to get through our days and check off the box of what needs to be done. Commitment from others is like autopilot for your vision as a leader.

Compliance is a low level of accomplishment.
#standtallstatement
Commitment from others is like autopilot for your vision as a leader.
#standtallstatement

Stand Tall Action

Share with your staff the reduce, not eliminate. Ask them how this concept connects to the following: Classroom Management, Parental Involvement, Teacher Involvement, Student Attendance, Student Discipline, Student Graduation, etc.

Stand Tall Ideas

Email Signature

Take a look at your outgoing email. Most people have an automatic signature that places your name and basic contact information at the end of every email. Some people get creative and add a motivational quote. This space is actually very valuable real estate. This space is an opportunity to let everyone you email know about something important. Think of your signature space as a place to showcase who you are, what you are doing, and how others can join in. Here are five ways to maximize your signature at the end of an email.

What Are You Up To?

Under your signature, list the dates of important events. If you are a classroom teacher, list the dates of the next big project, class trip, or parent visitation. As an administrator list report card dates, concert dates, or PTA/PTO meeting times. Update your information every other week. Over time, people will get use to looking for important information at the end of your emails.

The Links

Look for a great article that focuses on parent–child relationships or an article about the importance of schools in the community. Highlight a link under your signature. Not everyone will click the link, but some will. By doing this, you are continually sharing what is important to you and your school.

Color It Up!

Consider using different color font within your signature. It doesn't have to be a crazy hot pink. How about a burgundy or navy blue to highlight important information that you want others to know? Please, do not have three or four different colors. That would make it too difficult to read. Just pick one color and possibly bold a word or two that are important.

Contact Me!

Don't skimp on providing information about how to get in touch with you. Just because you are sending and receiving an email doesn't mean that is the only way to get back in touch. Within your signature, add the following:

Name

What you do in the school

Hours that you are available

Prep time

School address

School phone number

(Continued)

School fax number

Teacher website (active link)

School website (active link)

District website (active link)

School Facebook page (active link)

School Twitter name

If you offer this information at the end of every email, there is no way a parent can say they didn't know how to get a hold of you or you were not accessible.

Say Cheese!

If you are comfortable, consider adding a headshot under your signature. Simply cut and paste a nice, clear image of yourself. Do not use a full body image or a candid photo. You must appear professional and friendly. Also, be sure to shrink the image down to a sensible size. The photo should not be bigger than your typed name. If you don't want to use your photo, consider using the school's mascot. Again, the image should not be bigger than your typed name.

The focus of this idea is to increase communication and improve the image of the school. Through your email signature, you can continually share the vision of the school and maximize your public relations opportunities.

PS: I hope you are not planning to add every idea I shared with you into your email signature. Pick one or two that would work and try it out for a month or two. Let me know what your response is.

First Impression

When you walk into the front of your building, what do you see, hear, and smell? In most schools, you see a beige wall with a few posters or school projects hung on the wall. Possibly, a desk with someone who is checking in people for security reasons. You hear the rush of the traffic outside, a few students in the hallways, or possibly nothing at all. The smell could be many things. You could smell wet carpet from the runner in front of the door, the garbage from the can next to the wall, or the famous aroma of sweaty children.

Any way you look at it, the combination of sights and smells could make anyone entering the building have a not-so-good experience. When visitors enter your building, it is the first impression they get of what is important to the school. Don't leave this up to chance. Take a moment, stand outside of your building, walk in the front door, and let your senses take inventory. What is the message about your school when you enter? Is it a positive first impression? If the message isn't clear and you are not impressed, here are five ways to change that.

Plug In

If you walk in your building and get a whiff of the last sweaty child who walked by, consider using fresh-air plug-ins. Find an outlet or two that is close to the front door, get a few fragrant plug-ins, place the setting on low, and enjoy. Having a pleasant smell as you enter the building is a delightful surprise that goes a long way. *Make sure you change the plug-in monthly.*

Boom Box

Purchase a small Bluetooth speaker and place it near the main entrance. Create a playlist with classical music or familiar tunes and push play from a local computer or digital player. Make sure you put the playlist on repeat so the music will continually play. No need to turn the volume up to 10. Keep it at a level so people can notice the music when they enter. Having calming music play as people enter helps set the tone. This is especially helpful if you have an angry parent or community member coming in.

Say Cheese

Take several photos of students who attend the school. Pick out a few that are full of energy and have them enlarged to poster size. Frame the photos and arrange them in the lobby. Some people love black and white photos and some like the bright colors. Either way works well. The focus is to showcase what is most important, the students. Having student work on the walls is nice, but how often do you see people stopping to look at it? Displaying beautiful children on the walls will attract more people and make for a positive environment as you enter the school.

Theme

Place a large banner at the main entrance showcasing your theme for the year. The banner should clearly state what is important to everyone who enters. There is no doubt that the school is a positive place for learning.

Paperless

Get rid of all the paper taped to the front door. So often schools tape important messages to the front door. Here is a secret, NOBODY READS IT! Find another location to post those papers. If you must hang them at the front door, get some clear plastic sleeves and slide them into sleeves. That way they are straight, organized, and not ripped with tape hanging on it. Nothing says total confusion like a school door with 10 ripped announcements all over it.

Last Day Ice Cream

On the last day of school, after the students pull away on the buses, give your staff a treat. Schedule the local ice cream truck to come by the school that day and encourage each staff member to get one ice cream treat from the truck. This is a great way to say thank you for a great school year.

CHAPTER · THREE

Stand Tall Leaders Get Results

What is it that you want in your school? You want positive outcomes. You want results. It doesn't matter if it is related to student grades, classroom management, or team sports. That is partly why we do what we do. We are attempting to move others forward toward the expected outcomes and results. There are many different ways to try and get results. Within my conversations and consultations with multiple educational leaders they have shared different techniques, tricks and systems that are effective. Each of them is a small part of a bigger process and belief that we as leaders put into action.

3.1. The Results Formula

$$\frac{\textbf{Respect Recognize Reward + Reinforce}}{\textbf{Results}}$$

The results formula allows Stand Tall Leaders to get the results that they want. The results formula came from Jostens. Many educators are familiar with Jostens because they provide caps, gowns, rings, and yearbooks for schools throughout the country and abroad. A major focus of Jostens is to create items that enhance the memories that last in schools. To help with this they have a program called Jostens Renaissance®. Jostens Renaissance is all about improving the climate and culture in schools. Through that program they have developed the *Renaissance formula*. This results formula really does so much more than just guide the climate and culture of schools.

The Jostens results formula truly can give you the results that you want on many different levels. So, let's dig down into the results formula and how it can be applied, not only from a leadership standpoint, but also breaking it down into the classroom. The results formula consists of five words. Within the Jostens Renaissance world, they call it the five *R*s of Renaissance:

1. Respect
2. Recognize
3. Reward
4. Reinforce
5. Results

The first four *R*s allow the school or the classroom to truly get what it is that you want—results.

3.1.1. Respect

The first one of the five *Rs* is *respect*. What is it that you respect? What is important to you? What is important to the school? What is important to the classroom? If you were to take a survey of your school, the teachers, the students, the community, and you ask them what it is that you respect the most within the school, what answers would you get? You might get many different answers. You may get answers that are very similar, but not what you want.

When talking to higher-level administrators, superintendents, directors, I've found that they quote the mission statement or the vision statement as an example of what is respected in the school or district. There are many vision and mission statements out there that are absolutely wonderful, but can everyone in the school identify what that mission or vision statement is? Can they recite it? Does it truly identify what you respect in everything that you do on a daily basis? I would argue that usually, it's not. People cannot say the mission statement verbatim. They cannot truly get the full grasp of it, so therefore when you're identifying what it is you respect, I suggest that you identify those things very simply. It should be about four to five items that are clear and what you truly respect. Make them quick, easy, sensible statements that others can recite and remember. They don't even have to be statements. They could be just words. You can pull the words from the mission or vision statement. Pull a committee together to identify them. Do a survey. The goal is to identify what you respect that everyone can agree on and remember.

3.1.1.1. Internal Branding

Once you have what you respect clearly identified and agreed upon, it is important to ensure that you internally brand what you respect. Internally branding is all about being purposeful with how you are sharing information within the school community. Don't leave it up to chance that others will see, understand, and interact with the identified areas of respect. When a corporate company has a new product to hit the market, what does it do? It develops a marketing plan—the look of it, how is sounds, where it will be displayed, how often it is displayed, and how long it will be displayed. The company is attempting to grab the attention of people to want to be a part of the product or service.

Educators need to do the same thing. Think about when a new program or concept comes into a school. We announce it to those affected, provide some training, and hope that we get buy-in. What kind of branding and marketing is that?

3.1.1.2. *Branding with Purpose*

When developing what it is you respect, there needs to be a purposeful effort to brand it throughout the district/school/classroom. What to think about:

- How many things will it include?
- What does it look like?
- Where will it be posted?
- How often will we talk about it?
- When and how will we talk about it?

Identify what you respect and internally brand it throughout your school. #standtallstatement

3.1.1.2.1. *How Many Things Will It Include?*

Personally, I believe that you should focus on no more than four to five specific topics for respect. Beyond five topics people may not remember them. Keep in mind, the goal is for people to remember what you respect and live by them. If you have 20 different attributes that you respect, there is a high probability that you aren't going to remember them. Think specifically of what embodies the best attributes of the district/school/classroom. I'm sure there are some beliefs that can be blended together into one word or statement so that you do not have to have multiple words. Replace the classroom rules with what you respect. You can better connect with what you respect in the classroom. You cannot connect with rules and what you don't want in the classroom. Words or statements of respect in a classroom create a guiding belief system as opposed to rules that we live by. Seriously, does anyone truly live by those rules? Pick the four to five respect words or statements that are easy to remember and apply them to the lives of those in the school.

3.1.1.2.2. *What Does It Look Like?*

Think about some brands that are iconic within the world. *Ford, Apple, Coca-Cola, Disney*. Each of them has a specific look. You see it and immediately know what it means and what it stands for. Apple doesn't even have words, just an image. Each of these amazing companies has developed a powerful brand and image that is recalled the moment you see their names. The very same can take place within your district/school/classroom. Once you have identified what you respect, choose how it will look. What is the font? What order will the words be in? What color will it be? You want everyone to look at it and immediately remember what it stands for. This strengthens the purpose of it and the brand. Similar to a school mascot, it can embody a feeling or sense of understanding for a school culture, your list of what you respect can do the same thing.

3.1.1.2.3. Where Will It Be Posted?

Look throughout the campus to see where you will post the words/statements that you respect. The more locations, the better. By posting it in multiple locations you are increasing the probability that it will be seen and referenced. Yes, I know, over time it blends in with the wall and people don't see it. I always suggest that over winter break you ask the maintenance staff to move things around on the walls. It provides for a fresh look when people return and increases the possibility of it being seen. Where can you post it?

- Hallways and stairways
- Restrooms
- Classrooms and courtyards
- Offices and conference rooms
- Letterheads and email signatures
- Photo backdrops and bulletin boards
- Parking lot

Thinking of the classroom . . . Usually, educators post the rules of the classroom at the front of the room on a poster. Think differently and post what you respect on every wall of the classroom; not just the front. It increases the importance of your areas of respect and allows the teacher to reference them as he/she teaches. After all, they always tell teachers to "move around the room" during instruction. Now, when you reference what you respect, it is right next to you on the wall instead of just one location within the room.

3.1.1.2.4. How Often, When, and How Do We Talk About It?

Whenever you can! If there is any action done by anyone or event taking place it should be mentioned. There should not be a day that goes by when it isn't mentioned. Think about this:

- Morning and dismissal announcements
- Friday focus email

- Back-to-school night
- Parent and community meetings
- Board meetings
- Student assemblies
- Introductions

There are multiple opportunities to talk about what you respect. The goal is to be purposeful about it. Don't hope that someone brings it up. Develop a plan of when and where you will talk about it. Put it on the agenda for meetings and events. Clearly state that it is important, and you and others will make it happen.

The *how* is the emotion that is used when talking about what you respect. When talking about what the district/school/classroom respects, do not say it in a condescending way. It should not be said with an undertone of, ". . .here we go again." As the leader, take the time to be very clear with everyone about how it is to be discussed. If you are aware of others who are disrespecting what you respect through the way it is said, you need to call them on it.

Give what you respect a name. Meaning, title it so that it is memorable. Identify it as "The Top Five Things you Respect," "The Four Cornerstones of Respect," "The Three Keys of Respect." Basically, put some excitement to it. Maybe you can use the mascot in the name some way so that everybody understands what this is about. "The Cougar Paws of Respect," "The Lion Pride of Respect," "The Ravens Top Four Feathers of Respect." In the classroom, you can say these are "The Four Keys of Success" that we have in our classroom. You are trying to give it a name so that when people hear that name, they immediately think of all the areas you respect as a whole.

Whatever your items of respect might be, you're branding it by putting a title to them. The next step is to make sure that everybody knows what it is that you respect. This isn't a secret. Everyone knows it.

It is talked about the same way, so everybody understands that it is important. This is what we are about in this classroom, school, or district. Put it into the email signatures. Talk about it at district meetings. Post it in district buildings. Make it so that nobody can escape what you respect. It is everywhere.

Stand Tall Actions

Get a committee together of interested people and develop the items of respect. Also discuss what it will look like, where it will be posted and how it will be discussed.

3.1.2. Recognize

The second *R* is *recognize*. This means you are recognizing students and staff when they do what it is that you respect. What does recognize really mean? *Recognize* means that you are identifying people when they do a specific action. For this form of recognition you are not doing a big awards assembly. You are not giving out stickers or tickets. You are simply taking note and recognizing when people do what it is that you respect. When you recognize people when they do what it is that you respect, you are specifically outlining and strengthening the areas of respect that are most important to your school. You are moving closer to getting the results you want and need.

How do you recognize like this? By pointing out the person and saying things like,

- "Hey, way to go on number two. That's what we respect."
- "Oh, I see what's happening right here on number three of what we respect."
- "I appreciate what you did, that's right up the alley with number one."
- "I like that, it hits number five of our keys to success."
- "I see you. That's great what you did, just like number two of what we respect."

It doesn't take a lot of time or effort to recognize people when they do what you respect. The goal is taking the time to specifically outline and say something. When you say something, make sure you reference what number or specific item of what you respect they did. Now, I've heard many different things from people about why recognition would work or why recognition doesn't work. A lot of times people say they don't have time to do recognition. It takes less than a second to point out that someone's doing something well. Hey, way to go. Excellent job. . . and then you simply tag on what they're doing.

There are those educators who seem to thrive on pointing out when students and others are *not* doing the right thing. They feel an overwhelming need to find all the negative actions students do and pointing it out. I'm sure you can picture those individuals right now. My questions is this. . . Has that ever worked? Does it prevent the behavior for the long run? Does the probability of that student and others from doing bad behavior go down? Do others still do the same type of actions again and again? Yes! That continual behavior from educators doesn't even fall under the *reduce, not eliminate* concept. Pointing out students' faults continually doesn't reduce their behavior and will never eliminate. Now think of the other side of this. If you are continually pointing out the good that students are doing, specifically connected to what the positive attributes you respect in the school, what is the probability that behaviors will change? The probability of changing behaviors goes up considerably compared to the negative. When you recognize people for doing what you want them to do, other people take notice. As long as it is done equitably things will change.

Recognizing others when they do what you respect isn't just for students. As a Stand Tall Leader, when staff do the things that are connected to what you respect, it's as easy as taking a Post-It note, writing it down, and putting it on the teacher's desk or in their mailbox. You can pull them aside and say, Hey, I see what you're doing with number three. I really appreciate it so much. You're doing a great job with number four. During your faculty meetings, take the time to say, "...Hey, I saw this..., or I saw that..." Also, consider your Friday focus email that goes out to your staff. Highlight specific people and things that you saw that relate to what it is that you respect in that building. It is one thing to have the students get recognized for doing what you respect, but it is a much bigger thing to recognize the staff when they do what you respect. It strengthens and empowers them to follow suit and do the same to the students.

When you see students in the hallway and they're doing what it is you respect, you must take note of it and recognize. When you recognize, make sure you reference the specific action. If you don't know what action it is, don't worry—it should be hanging on a walk close by. Remember, you posted it EVERYWHERE within the building. Just look to the right or left and it should be there to reference. "Hey, way to go on number four." If you see them in a classroom or out on the field or wherever it might be, you take that time to give that recognition. Remember, it's not just you as a Stand Tall Leader recognizing others. It needs to be a practice from everyone! At a district level, you push the recognition out to all areas of the district. Create a culture around core principles that are exhibited continually, even if it's maintenance or an area that is not directly connected to students. "Hey, you're really hitting what we are all about and respect." That's one of the things that's most important to this district, and if you've properly branded it by identifying what it is that you respect, it is clearly posted everywhere throughout the district. So when you mention it, it's very easy to connect to it, focus on it, and look at it, so others know exactly what the expectations are.

As a Stand Tall Leader in the classroom, as the students start to do things that you want them to do, you should be identifying what you respect. It takes very little time to point out what a student is doing right. You can continually recognize students all the time with this. It is not that hard to do. The key is to remember to do it. You have to make it a habit to identify what it is you respect. As you know, there are students who are not going to behave. Many teachers take plenty of time to recognize poor behavior that goes against what is respected in the classroom. Wouldn't you rather use that energy and time to recognize the behaviors that you want to see in the classroom?

When you see students in the hallway and they're doing what it is you respect, you must take note of it and recognize.
#standtallstatement

Nighttime DJ Voice

Daytime DJ Voice

I know you have listened to the radio before. Maybe you have your favorite morning or daytime DJ personality. Mine was the Tom Joyner Morning Show. He and his crew would tell jokes, bring up silly topics, and laugh all morning long. I would wonder how in the world could they be so happy, so early in the day? Nevertheless, listening to them would put me in a better mood. I would feel like I today would be a good day.

On the other hand, I had my favorite nighttime DJ. Back in the day that was Tony Brown. Tony had a deep, mellow soft voice. It sounded like he was in a recliner sipping on his favorite drink as he played the soft tunes for me. I could feel myself winding down for the evening. I would be shocked that Tony Brown didn't fall asleep on the air every night.

Think about student recognition and the use of your own daytime DJ voice and your nighttime DJ voice. How are you using those voices when addressing students? Over my 25+ years in education I've come to realize that most educators use the daytime DJ voice when addressing students who are NOT doing what they are supposed to and using the nighttime DJ voice when students ARE doing what they are supposed to. Isn't that backward? Please, read that sentence again. . .

Think about this. . . A student is in the classroom out of her seat and not doing her work. The teacher jumps on her case using the daytime DJ voice to get her to comply with what the rules. The student sees that her actions are getting the teacher hyped up and resists. After this continues for the next four to five minutes, the student sits down. Once the student sits down and starts to work the teacher might stop by her desk and say "good job" using her nighttime DJ voice.

Think about this. . . Same student is in the classroom out of her seat and not doing her work. The teacher addresses the student's behavior using the nighttime DJ voice to get her to comply with the rules. The student sees that her actions have no effect on the teacher's mood. She tries once more with no outcome and sits down. Once the student sits down and starts to work the teacher stops by her desk and says "good job" using her daytime DJ voice.

Looking at each scenario, what has a higher probability of continual success?

The only time students should see adults getting hyped up with the daytime DJ voice is for good things. All negative things need to be handled at the lowest emotional level using the nighttime DJ voice. The outcomes will be so much better over time. Additionally, it enhances and strengthens what it is you respect.

Stand Tall Action

Try for one week using your daytime DJ voice when students do what your respect and your night-time DJ voice when students are not doing what you respect.

3.1.3. Reward

The third *R* is *reward.* I get it, some people have issues with giving people rewards for good behavior or doing the right thing. I get it, there are those out there who say that it needs to be only internal rewards. People have to want to do well. Although with this formula it just doesn't work without some kind of reward system to anchor the efforts people do. But setting up a reward system it truly motivates, inspires, and gives people the drive to continue to do what it is that you respect. Setting up a reward system specifically connected to what it is that you respect is vital to the success of getting the Results that you are looking for. When you're setting up this reward system, you are clearly identifying what the reward will be. How it connects directly to what you respect and when it's going to take place.

3.1.3.1. No Surprise Awards!

NO SURPRISE REWARDS! Don't try to hide the rewards or make up rewards that others don't know about. Make sure the rewards are public. Make sure the reward criteria are public. Make sure the timeline for the reward is public. If people know exactly what the reward will be, when it's going to take place and it is directly connected to the agreed upon areas of respect, there is no room for argument. You know how it goes, there will always be critics with the school. The critics will always questions why someone got the reward. They will question the criteria to get the reward. They will think that there are favorites to get the reward. Prevent the critics from being critical. Make sure everyone knows what they are earning. That's right, they are *earning* that reward. This is not bribery. This is not "catch them being good." It's, "You did it! Congratulations! You followed the clearly defined expectation, so here is your earned reward." It's *earning* a reward not *getting* a reward.

No Surprise Rewards! #standtallstatement

It's important that you have a reward system that matches what it is that you really want to have happen in your district, school, or classroom. Identify to everyone early on when the

Stand Tall Idea

Reward Wall

Within every school should be a reward wall. The reward wall isn't to showcase the students who got rewards, but a display of every possible reward that could be achieved within that building. Each display of the reward includes criteria for how to get that specific reward. Additionally, provide the timeline of when that reward will be given and recognized. Three things happen if this is done:

1. Students will be able to see what is obtainable within that school. Students can now start to set goals toward achieving the awards that fit them best. Their learning and actions can be more focused toward outcomes if they connect directly to what you respect within the school.
2. Critics lose their voice. Those who would usually question why certain students get a reward and complain that rewards have no merit don't have an argument. Any complaint from the critic can be silenced by pointing to the criteria. To the critics it changes from getting a reward to earning merit.
3. It strengthens what you respect. Once all the rewards are posted, you can start to see if all the rewards move forward what you respect in your school. Some rewards might need to be altered. Some rewards need to happen more often. Some rewards might need to go away. You may also find that there is a population within the school that is not being represented.

Once you have your reward wall, you need to reference it at least once a month in meetings, communication, to the students, to the community. Make it a practice to use it regularly. You can have it electronically as well, but make sure it is a living wall within your school.

recognition will take place. Pull out your calendar and pick the dates and times that work best and put it into the calendar so everyone can see and know. Think about this:

- Are you going to do recognition every month in your faculty meeting?
- Are you going to do it every month over the announcements?
- Are you going to do recognition once a marking period?
- Are you going to do recognition every week in the classroom?
- Are you going to do it every other week in the classroom?

If you have the four keys of what you respect posted everywhere within the school, you recognize those exact four keys. I am not a fan of surprise recognitions. Especially when you are starting a new recognition system or program. Recognition needs to happen when people know what it is, they are working toward. When students and staff get recognized for doing the right thing, they should feel confident. They should think, "I've done exactly what is expected of me. Yes, I've put in the work. Yes, I've exhibited the behaviors that I'm supposed to be exhibiting." And now others notice what I have done. It should not be, "Who me? Did I do that? Oh man, I really did behave that way? Oh, wow, they actually followed through?" It should not be a surprise that people get recognized.

3.1.3.2. What Is a Reward?

What you actually give as the reward varies greatly. Rewards do not have to be elaborate. Rewards do not have to be over the top. Rewards just have to mean something to the person receiving it. It is a physical item that represents the meaning of what you respect. Some of the best rewards I've seen are stickers. Kids love stickers! People love stickers. It's something that they can hold onto. They can put it onto things, they can collect them. It is a bonus if they look fun or they smell great. People love them. Think about football players in college. There are several college football teams out there that place stickers on the helmets of players when they do a great job as a reward. Those players will kill on that football field to receive a sticker. Just a little sticker! Is that crazy or what? It's not about what it is as much as what it means. Therefore, identify what the reward is going to be that you're going to provide and "stick" with it.

Is it going to be stickers every other week or every week? Is it going to be a certificate of some sort? Is it going to be a medal? When it comes to giving rewards, there is something called VTW. VTW comes from the Jostens Renaissance program.

VTW:
VISIBLE:
Catchy to the eye. Shiny, colorful, or a familiar image.

TANGIBLE:
Something they can hold on to. Worthy of keeping in a safe place or collecting over time.

WALK-AROUNDABLE:
Something that you can walk around with and show off. When people run a race and get a medal, they want to walk around and show it off so others can see. That is what makes them proud of their accomplishments. Others can then say congratulations, good job!

School swag, T-shirts, hats, scarves, metals. If you're going to give stickers, get some stickers that they can stick on something and collect them and walk around with it. Magnet, fun school stuff that and strengthens your school brand, strengthens what it is that you are identifying as what you respect. Look for those rewards that connect directly to what it is you respect.

A reward is a physical item that represents the meaning of what you respect. #standtallstatement

3.1.4. Reinforcement

The next *R* is all about *reinforcement*. If you were to go to Google images and type in the word *reinforcement*, you would see images of building scaffolding. If you notice in these pictures, there is not *one* metal bar holding everything together. There are *many* metal bars that hold up the framing of a building and securing the concrete. So therefore, that leads me to think that in order to do *reinforcement*, you have to do the first three *R*s again and again and again and again and again, and then when you're done with that, you do it again and again and again. Then after that, again and again and again!

Many times a program is introduced in a school, and as soon as it starts, the teachers start rolling their eyes and saying, "This will be gone soon." Then guess what? It's gone soon. When you have a new mindset like the results formula, where you are identifying what it is you respect to recognizing people when they do what you respect and then you're rewarding them for what they do, are you expecting it to be scheduled? You need to make sure that it is done consistently. It does not stop. It happens again and again and again and again. When you have scheduled rewards, make sure you follow up with those rewards. Have the INTEGRITY to make sure that it happens. Remember, *keep your promises and do what you say you are going to do*! Not another One and Done. Educators are used to that, and they hate it.

If you want to recognize district staff for what you respect, you need to make sure that it gets done with fidelity. Set a schedule, figure out a time, do whatever you have to do to make it happen. It is vitally, vitally important that the recognition and rewards take place every single time. Reinforce what it is that you want to have happen throughout the district regularly. Internally brand what you respect so that it is strong within the fabric and the fibers of your school or district or classroom. Make sure that it is everywhere.

Now think about it. If you clearly identified what it is that you *respect,* and it is internally branded and showcased everywhere throughout your school, district, or classroom. You are *recognizing* students and staff constantly when they do what it is that you *respect* and what is important in your school, district, or classroom. Students and staff all know that you see them doing the right thing. Then you have a reward system that's connected directly to what it is that you respect, and they know when the reward is. *No Secret Rewards!* Everyone knows exactly what needs to happen and they can see what it takes to earn the reward. Everyone knows that they actually will get rewarded the way that you said that they would because it's reinforced by you saying what you respect over and over again.

3.1.5. Results

If you implement the first four *R*s, will you get the *results* that you want? YES, YOU WILL GET THE RESULTS THAT YOU WANT! Remember: Reduce, not eliminate. It's all about increasing probability of things to change for the better. Increasing the probability of people changing their behaviors. Increasing the probability of changing their actions so that they can fit within what it is that you respect is higher than if you did nothing and just hoped that everyone saw the mission statement or vision statement and lived up to it. There is a difference! This is how you make a change! That's how you strengthen what it is that you have in your school in your district, in your classroom. Get the results that you want.

YES, YOU WILL GET THE RESULTS THAT YOU WANT!
#standtallstatement

3.1.5.1. Using the Results Formula: Who Has the Best Question?

Here is an example of how the *results formula* works. Years ago, when I was a building principal, I had the superintendent come to the building principals and talk about rigor.

If you spent any time in education, you know about rigor. Back in the day it was the big buzzword in education. The superintendent preached about how to improve the rigor in the classrooms and in the schools. Rigor, rigor, rigor, get those teachers to ask higher-level questions, make it happen! As the building principal, I started to think about what we could do in order to make it better and have the teachers ask higher-level questions. Instead of going to another professional development and having the teachers roll their eyes and feel guilty because they're not asking higher level questions every single day we decided to implement the *results formula* as it relates to asking better questions. The difference is, we switched it and put it on to the students. The teachers were going to ask the students to ask better questions in class. We called it, "Who Has The Best Question?"

We started by identifying what we *respect* by saying to students that we want them to ask better questions. That's what we respect. We respect students asking great questions. We decided on the look and color of the "Who Has The Best Question?" logo and created a nice fun design. We posted that logo everywhere. *Internal branding.* It was in the hallways, it was in the bathrooms, it was in the classrooms, it was in the stairwells. We talked about it during morning announcements. "Do you have the best question in class? Can you give the best question to the teachers about what you're learning? We want the best questions from you."

Along with the *internal branding,* each classroom received the bin. If a student asked a great question, the teachers would recognize the student who asked the question. If it was a really great question the student would write down the question with their name on a card and put it in the bin. At the end of the month, each class would have a reward ceremony to identify the best question of the month. They would pull out all of the questions for the month and the students in the classroom would vote which question was the best question of the month? The identified student would get a *VTW Reward.*

We started doing this. Everybody was on board. We created our logo. We branded it everywhere. We talked about it. The teachers are starting to look for students who are asking the best questions. Guess what happened? We ended up with a bunch of dumb questions from the students. The students would go out of their way to ask questions that were not the top-end questions. The questions were all over the place. They asked questions about science in the middle of social studies. They were asking questions about language arts, doing math. They were reaching and stretching all over the place to get these questions. The teachers said, this isn't working. I don't think this is going to work. We looked at the previous *R*, which is *reinforce.* We had to reinforce our actions and keep it going again and again and again. Therefore, we agreed, when students ask questions that were not connected or related to what it is that the teachers were looking for, which is what we *respect,* we basically ignored them. "Sorry, that's not the type of questions we were looking for. . ." and then kept it going. Using our nighttime DJ voice. Eventually, students started asking quality questions. The teachers were told to go above and beyond when they saw a student ask a great question. Using their daytime DJ voice to hype up the question.

The teachers said things like, "Wow. I think that was a great question." "Great question, what do you think everybody?" When that happened, the students wrote the questions down on paper, put their name to it, put it in the bin, and then the teacher moved on with the instruction focusing on that great question. Over time, we started to notice that students started really digging down and finding the best questions that relate to the instruction that was given. The questions got better and better each month. We would take the time out at the end of the month to identify the students who had the best questions for the month. For the reward at the end of the month, we simply took a question mark stamped out on the Ellison machine, placed it onto some heavier colored construction paper and gave it to the student. We wrote at the top, "Best Question of the Month" and the name of the month and the student's name on it. That's it! That was the reward. The students loved it. Some of the students would walk around with it in a hallway holding it up. They would put it in their lockers. They would hold on to it. They would take it home. That basic piece of paper with a question mark on it gave the students some pride for their accomplishments.

At the end of each marking period, we would have a school-wide award ceremony to celebrate academic and behavior success. We would take all the winners from each month leading up to that time and have a small committee pick the top two questions for the marking period. We would highlight those two students at the awards assembly and then really go over to top with a reward. We would give a great trophy or certificate, or a banner of names hung up for the best question. It was sponsored by our school PTA.

What happens when students ask better questions? The other students are listening more to the instruction because they want to know the answer to that great question. Additionally, when students ask better questions, who else starts asking better questions? That's right. Teachers have to start asking better questions because you have to improve your game along with what the students are doing. Teachers were even coming back saying that the questions are so good, "I don't know if I can answer them." My response was good. Turn it back to the students. "Oh, that's a great question. You other two students, you look that up and find the answer to that." Now they're doing investigation and deeper inquiry.

Instruction is improving and rigor started to go up. We saw the results in our test scores. We saw the results in the grades, we saw results in the students' answers. We saw the results in our benchmark testing, and we saw the results from the parent's responses. All because we implemented the results formula. We simply identified what we *respect,* which is higher-level questions from the students. We *recognized* the students when they asked higher level questions. We *rewarded* the students at the end of each month and at the end of the marking period for the very best questions. And then we *reinforced* it because we didn't give up. We kept identifying students with the best questions. When we did that, we ended up with the results that we wanted, which was a higher level of rigor throughout the school. The **results formula works!**

Stand Tall Action

Identify a wall or bulletin board in your school that is seen by everyone. Post every single reward and recognition. Post how to get every single reward and recognition. Post when people can receive every single reward and recognition. Once the display is done, talk about the display at least once a week during announcements.

Watch what happens!

Stand Tall Ideas

Hello, Thank You for Calling!

When parents and community call the main number of the school what do they hear? It is usually the school secretary saying something like, ". . .thank you for calling Great Run School. Please listen closely, for the following options have changed. Press one for the cafeteria. . ." It is usually the same message for every school. Nothing differentiates you from any other school of business in the country. Consider updating the message. Instead of the same message as every other school, here are some ideas of how to personalize your message.

Use Your Students

Find a student who has a great voice and can speak well. Write a script that clearly states what you want people to know when they call. Practice with the students to make sure he/she has it right. When recording the outgoing message with the student, remind the student to smile. You can hear if someone is smiling. It makes the message more pleasant and people are more receptive. Also, if you have an angry parent calling into the school ready to "go off" on a teacher or administrator, hearing a happy child welcome them to the school may help calm them down before speaking to an adult.

Theme and Goals

Start the outgoing message by clearly stating the theme for the school year or a major goal for the school. This clearly outlines what you are about. It does not have to be a long, drawn-out statement. Just a quick mention of what the school is focusing on for the year. It would be even better if the school principal says the statement.

Slow Down

Nothing is more frustrating than calling a school or business and hearing a voice ramble through the options at lightning speed. Remember, the person calling the school is trying to process what is said. Just like when you listen to a message that was left for you and the person leaves the phone number as if it were a race. You have to rewind the message two or three times in order to make sure it is correct (oh come on, I'm not the only one who does that). The same is when people call in to the school and listen to the outgoing message. Many times, they just give up and press "0" for the main office or operator. It's just not worth listening to it again. Whoever leaves the message needs to slow down so the caller can process what is being said.

Dates

If you are able to change your outgoing message easily, consider providing the dates to important school events. As you know, many parents and community call in order to get clarification on events and times. Cut down on the number of calls by providing the information ahead of time. Remember to change the message once the event is over.

Thank You Day

Thank You Day is the last Thursday of each month. On that day every student and staff member in the school writes a thank you to someone else in the building. The letters can go to other students or staff. To keep the focus on writing, the students must use proper letter-writing technique. The grade level determines how much the student is to write. Some classes base their writing on a picture prompt. At the end of that Thursday, a small group of staff organizes the thank you letters. On Friday morning, the principal delivers the letters to the classrooms for the students and staff.

You should see the excitement in the students' eyes as they get letters. It is even a better pick-me-up for the staff. You never know how thankful people are for the little things you do.

As the principal, each month on Thank You Day I give a heartfelt thank you to several staff members. I present the *thank you* in front of their class or group. The staff member is extremely happy and posts the thank you in their room.

Thank You Day improves the writing skill of the students, provides recognition to those who deserve it, and best of all, costs nothing!

3.1.5.2. State of the Union Address

Every American president does a State of the Union Address. The focus of that address is to share with the country the "State of the Union." What does the president talk about?

- How we are doing.
- What concerns there may be.
- Assurance that the Union is okay.
- Getting people excited about what is to come.
- Rallying everyone around a cause or need.

Basically, it is supposed to refocus the country on a specific vision and goals. The success of the State of the Union Address is arguably due to the immense size of the country. Nevertheless, it is expected and for the most part looked forward to by Americans.

The same concept should be true for district and building leadership. At least once or twice a year, hold a State of the Union Address. A great time to have it is either at the start of each marking period or when returning from winter break or spring break. When I did this, my school mascot was the Hartford Hounds. Therefore, I called it the State of the Hound Address. All students and staff assembled together, and I provided two main areas of focus:

1. Data and information about what we just did and what is to come
2. Motivation and refocusing on the values of the school

The data and information that was shared was divided into grade levels and teams. I would share grade point average data, discipline data, grade level testing, and growth expectancy. However, when the data and information was shared, it was done in a way that was age appropriate and didn't put anyone specifically on blast or praise. This wasn't an awards ceremony or public flogging. I would use a PowerPoint and school branding images throughout the presentation. All data that was shared was given to the teachers so they could discuss in the classrooms if they wished later. The information shared would talk about the success of previous events and upcoming events that we are looking forward to. The focus is to not use negative language when discussing upcoming events. Please don't start barking about how poor behavior will prevent students from attending. Instead, state what positive behaviors would allow students to attend.

Motivation should be a major part of the State of the Union. Be sure to have time to highlight great accomplishments that connect to the vision and expectations of the district/school. If you have respect statements, mission statement, or a mantra, be sure to state these. Better yet, have everyone stand and say it together. Remember, the goal is to strengthen the Union. Share examples of how actions of groups within the school have showcased the vision. At times I have found short video clips that strengthen the vision. Refocus everyone on the beliefs, values and actions that you want to depend on.

This can be done at every level within the district. As a superintendent, don't do this only at a board meeting. Depending on the district, most people don't attend board meetings. Pick a day and location within the district and send out invites to the staff. It will mean so much more to them if it is done this way. As a subject supervisor, do this with your department. Many supervisors are close to those within the department and would tend to make the State of the Union Address more casual. I encourage you not to do that. Keep it formal and serious. It will strengthen the message. At the building level, it is very effective. You will instantly feel a difference in the building immediately following the address.

The most important part of the State of the Union Address is for the LEADER to give the address. Don't let ANYONE ELSE TALK! Only you do it. This establishes you as the leader of the school/district. Remember, leaders are not supposed to blend in. Put your big girl panties on and be the Stand Tall Leader. Use your resources and supports to properly prepare your presentation. Practice, Practice, Practice: Especially if you are not the best public speaker. Reach out to your "go-to" teachers and staff for support. If you want people to applaud at certain spots, let them know ahead of time so they can get it going. You got this!

3.2. Don't Let a Good Crisis Go to Waste

When you initially hear this, it sounds rather cold and heartless. The first time I heard it, I didn't really get it. Who in the world wants a crisis to take place, and how are you going to let a crisis not go to waste? It sounds like you are setting your organization up to fail. It sounds kind of greedy or selfish. Basically, you are saying, I'm going to get something out of a crisis. That just doesn't sound right.

During my experience as a principal and a superintendent, I've come to realize that crises happen no matter what, and you have to do the best you can to prevent the crisis from happening to begin with. You have to get the most that you can out of a crisis once it happens. While a crisis is taking place, you are not necessarily going to get anything out of it, but some good things can come out of the proper reflection and understanding from that crisis. Maybe something was overlooked or did not take place that caused this crisis to take place to start with. Sometimes a crisis is completely out of your hands, as with a natural disaster or pandemic like COVID-19. If you are not going to learn and benefit your organization from the event in some way, then you will not be the Stand Tall Leader that you claim that you are. Nobody wants to have a crisis take place. The goal is to make sure you do the best that you can and learn from it when it does. To start, you need to understand the benefits of a crisis.

3.2.1. A Crisis Causes the Best and the Worst in Us to Come Out

When the worst comes out in you, it's like pouring hot metal. The impurities of that hot metal rise to the top to be skimmed off. That's kind of what happens when a crisis takes place. It's like you are that molten hot metal being poured out in your actions, and all the worst and bad material that's inside comes to the forefront. The crisis is an opportunity to skim off those negatives and that waste. Identify what did not go well with your actions. What are the deep-rooted issues and concerns that come to the forefront during a crisis that you can then skim off, handle, and get rid of?

Learn from your mistakes. The best thing that you can do is practice the best that is within you. Let the best that you practice come out within you instead of the worst. As you practice throughout your times where there is not a crisis, is that is your best? What you're practicing? Because that's what's really going to come to the top. Come on, you know this. It's just like how you practice fire drills in your school. The drills are practiced when there isn't a fire, so that if there is a fire it becomes automatic

The crisis is an opportunity to skim off those negatives and that waste. #standtallstatement

behavior. It then won't be the impurities or the negative things that are within you. You want the very best so that you don't have to skim them off the top. But if you do, skim them off the top and get rid of them. Recognize your frustrating situations, and from them you develop new habits and actions.

3.2.2. A Crisis Rearranges Your Priorities

I'm sure most everyone has seen the movie *The Bucket List* with Morgan Freeman and Jack Nicholson. They realize that they are going to die, and because of that they've created a list of things that they must do, and they're putting it in a bucket. When a crisis takes place, it does rearrange your priorities as to what is most important.

Their life was going along fine, but then when this crisis took place, they rearranged it and identified what's most important. Then they went for it. Once they knew things changed, they rearrange their priorities. A crisis provides clarity of what's really important. A lot of times we get caught up into the daily going on and the daily situations of a job or a position. The daily things that you do and what you think is important isn't really important. But when a crisis takes place, that's when you realize what really is important in the list of priorities of what you believe. A crisis puts in perspective what you think is right and how are you going to act, shift, and change. During and after a crisis, you need to take that time to review what's really most important and change priorities.

3.2.3. A Crisis Increases Your Capacity to Discover and Leverage Your Gifts and Talents

There are gifts and talents that we did not know that we had until a crisis takes place. As stated before, what you practice comes out within you. It is important that you know that those gifts and talents are what you need to continue to practice. Those talents are the ones that may come out as long as you've been practicing them. You can call on your many different talents and gifts when a crisis arises. It increases the capacity to discover and leverage those gifts. In the movie *Apollo 13* there was a moment where the engineers needed to create and design a CO_2 pump from the materials available on the ship. They pulled the knowledge and the gifts of all those around them to create something brand new. There was a crisis, but because they had these gifts and talents and knowledge, they were able to find the solution. When a crisis is taking place, as long as you are trained, continually improving yourself, and are aware of the talents and gifts that you have, then these will come forward as opposed to those negative areas that eventually need to be skimmed off the top.

You have many different talents and gifts that you can call on when a crisis arises. #standtallstatement

3.2.4. A Crisis Identifies the Critical Importance of Community

Nobody wants to be alone in a crisis. Most call on those close to you to support you and develop unity through the crisis. The decisions are stronger with others during a crisis. It reassures you that the decisions you are making and the people who are affecting the decisions mean something and have value. Many times, when a crisis takes place, you may be the one who is leading the charge, but others come around to offer support to make sure that the best decisions can be made. Sometimes the people you wouldn't think would be there are there, and the people who you thought would be there are not there. Be very aware of who is there and who is *not* there for you during times of crisis. That says a lot about who they are and their allegiance and focuses for the organization. A crisis can identify who your true supporters are.

3.2.5. Crisis Example: Mississippi Schools after Hurricane Katrina

Back on August 29, 2005, Hurricane Katrina hit landfall directly on top of Biloxi, Mississippi. Everything was destroyed, including the Pascagoula-Gautier School District. Prior to Hurricane Katrina, the school district had average to below-average buildings, technology, and grounds. When Hurricane Katrina hit the Gulf Coast, it leveled the buildings, materials, and grounds within the district. As upsetting as it was to have such a horrible tragedy take place, Superintendent Wayne Rodolfich saw the opportunity to rebuild the Pascagoula-Gautier School District to make it a hundred times better than what they had before. The district partnered with JBHM Architects to recreate a better district from the ground up.

Superintendent Rodolfich stated that the goal was "to create the most modern environment for children to attend schools with the greatest diversity of opportunity for our students." The Pascagoula-Gautier School District was able to rebuild with state-of-the-art technology and materials, create a new performing arts center, and enhance the community overall.

They understood the value of not letting a crisis go to waste.

3.3. Get It When You Don't Get It

You get it when you don't get it. One of the best ideas that we ever came up with was when we started to showcase the students who got straight *A*'s and made the honor roll at the end of each quarter. We used the poster-making machine at the end of each marking period to type up a list of students who got straight *A*'s and *A*'s and *B*'s. We hung the posters in the hallways so that the students could see who earned the recognition.

The very first time that we did this for our students, it went over great. The students were running up to the posters, identifying their name, sharing the excitement that they had with each other. It was awesome. The next day after we put up the posters, a mother of one of the students came to the school very upset. She pointed to the posters and said, "These need to come down. My daughter is very upset about this." We were concerned that we wrote her name wrong or we forgot to include her name. The mother stated that her daughter was very upset because her name was not up there, because she did not make honor roll or straight-A list. We needed to take them all down because her daughter and other students who didn't make the honor roll and straight-A list were embarrassed. She stated that there were too many students having a problem with it. My response to her was, "Seriously, *nobody's* supposed to be recognized because your daughter is upset and didn't make the grade to get on the board?"

The mother responded, "That's not what I'm saying."

"So what are you saying? What is it that you expect me to do? *Nobody's* supposed to get recognized because she didn't do it? That just doesn't make sense."

The mother continued on to say that she's just upset, her daughter is embarrassed, and it's hard for her to face her friends because of it. We stated that we are not changing anything. Mom said that she was going to take it above my head. We were very happy to give her directions on how to go to central office. I will easily defend recognizing students any day of the week.

The next marking period, we posted the grades again. Guess whose name was on the list? That right. That girl's name was on the list. Not just honor roll. She got straight *A*'s. You see, sometimes when it comes to recognition and becoming motivated, *You Get It When You Don't Get It.* When someone *doesn't get* the recognition or reward, that's when *they get it.* That moment when they are left out is when it sinks in. That is when they understand what is necessary to get to that next level and get the recognition that others are getting and they are not. Some people are hardheaded. Some people don't get things right away. Even though you tell them, they have to go through something in order to *get it.*

Sometimes recognition is difficult. It is hard because there are those who are very close to getting the recognition but didn't make it. When they don't get that level of recognition, the goal is for them to step up and do what is necessary to get the recognition the next time. This is why we say, *No Secret Rewards!* Ensuring that it is very public what the recognition and rewards are and how to achieve them is vital. By having the recognition and rewards public, it reduces the probability of criticism and the argument of people saying I didn't know.

Growing up as a young boy, there were times that my parents gave me direction of what I needed to do or how I could be successful. I didn't always pay attention to them. I thought that I knew what I needed to do. They didn't know what they were talking about. I'm sure you had the same experience. Because of not listening, life was a little hard in some areas. Because I didn't *get it*, that's when I *got it.* When I didn't get those successes that I thought I was going to get. When I didn't get the advancements that I thought it was going to get. When I didn't get all the great things that I thought I was going to get. That's when I "got it." Once I got it, then I knew what I needed to do to adjust, change, and to make myself better.

That's how life works. That's how recognition should work. That's how learning and growth happen in schools. As a Stand Tall Leader, you need to understand that sometimes those around you will only get it when they don't get it. You can give the direction, you can give the advice, you can guide them to the path they want to go, but ultimately, people are people, students are students, teachers are teachers, parents are parents. They have the will to make their own decisions and choose their own outcomes. At times when they don't get what it is that they need to get, that's when they are going to ultimately get it.

This is why I keep stressing, No Secret Rewards. If you make sure that all rewards are public, fair, and clearly showcased, there will be no excuse for those who don't get the reward to complain or say they didn't know. True, they may think that it's not fair. They may think that they've been wronged, but as long as you have provided a clear explanation of what is needed to get the recognition or reward, you can defend the decision and merit of that reward. To be honest, ensuring that there are No Secret Rewards allows others to earn the reward instead of being given the reward. Truthfully, that is the best defense to those who don't "get it" at first. Whatever the recognition or reward is has criteria attached to it, and making sure everyone knows that criteria allows everyone an equal shot at following through with the criteria and EARNING the reward.

Hold true to your criteria and allow some people to fail in order to improve. Some of the greatest advancements that I've made in my life are from when I've failed, when I make the wrong decision, and when I've missed out. Think back into your time as an educator. The lessons that you've learned the most are probably those areas where you didn't do well or you saw someone else not do well.

Someone has failed when they are unable to move to the next level. Make the necessary adjustments so when you do get it, the recognition means so much more. I don't know anyone who has improved significantly without some level of pain and discomfort. It's a part of life. It's part of the process and understanding that moves you to the next level as a Stand Tall Leader.

Think about the times that you've had awards assemblies, or you had some type of recognition in your school. When giving out the awards to those students who earned the award, you look out and you see some of those students who just didn't make the mark, and you feel sad for them. You feel like you want to do more for them, and you want to be able to get them to the level of recognition that you know they can reach. Not getting it is what's necessary for them to get it.

As a Stand Tall Leader, step up and share with others what the process is. Explain what it takes to get to that next level, what it means to get it when you don't get it. That's the mark of a Stand Tall Leader.

You Get It when you don't Get It!
#standtallstatement

Stand Tall Ideas

I Blew It, Knew It, Learned Through It

Be vulnerable and share with your staff what you did that was a huge mess-up. After sharing how you messed up, share what you learned from the mess-up. When the leader shows how she grew from the mistakes, others will feel empowered to embrace their blunders. Do this a few times a year. Possibly have a spot within your weekly email to share this. Consider using multiple locations to showcase this (meetings, blogs, video, articles, email, etc.).

Comeback Kid

Within my school we wanted to ensure that we recognized as many students as possible. We noticed that some students just don't make it academically. We also noticed that those students as well as others do improve. Therefore, we came up with the Comeback Kid recognition.

In order to be a Comeback Kid, a student moves up at least one grade level in any subject area. A student can move up from a B to an A or from an F to a D. Any move up makes the mark. Throughout the second marking period we advertised the concept of Comeback Kid. The second marking period is best because they would have one set of grades as a starting point. Our advertisement for Comeback Kid was a photo of a student with a towel cape standing like a superhero. We talked about it during morning announcements every other day. We had posters all over the school. We sent notes and messages home through text and phone calls. The hype around the Comeback Kid was huge!

Every teacher wrote the name of each student who moved up one grade level in any subject. During the rally, each Comeback Kid was announced and given a multicolored wrist band that had Comeback Kid on it. All the names of the Comeback Kids were posted in the hallways. We only posted the name and not the grade they moved up. With the wristband, teachers and students commented on the accomplishment.

The energy around improving and doing your best was contagious. Students were doing all they could to get the wristband and recognition. The next marking period, it was a different color wristband. It is a silly advertisement and gimmick. Regardless of what it is, it worked! Grades went up and learning increased, all for a wristband and recognition as a Comeback Kid.

Failing Forward Award

Give an award to students or staff who failed at something, learned from it, and then came out on top.

3.4. Hallway Brand

Every time you walk past someone in your building or district, you are reinforcing the brand within your school. That's something I heard from a friend of mine, Dr. Phil Campbell. It is so true. As a leader in the building, every time you walk past someone you are reinforcing what's important to your school. I get it, there are times that you are walking around and you have things going on in your mind, or you are figuring out and issue in your head, or you are on a mission to get somewhere and you just don't have time to stop and have long conversations with everyone. That's not what I'm talking about. What I'm talking about is your body language, your quick statement, the daily actions that are said and done by you every day. How are you strengthening what you respect each and every day?

One of the things that I would always do whenever I went into the hallways of the school is to make it a point to do a Stand Tall movement in order to get myself prepared. I would simply raise my shoulders up, push my shoulders back, and then pushed my shoulders down. By doing this quick little motion, it allowed me to have my chest out, moved my head up, and my shoulders are back. It appeared as if I knew what I was doing and I had confidence. I also made it a point to always smile. I would naturally have a smile on my face anyway, but I made it a point to increase my smiling every day. When I first started doing this, my face hurt and I started to think, this doesn't mean anything. Nobody really cares. But over time I would hear from people that Mr. Bollar is always happy. Mr. Bollar likes what he does. Mr. Bollar always notices you. Those little things mean something, especially when you're the leader in the building. How often do you smile?

Tall people don't blend in. Playing hide and seek usually ends with a tall person being it. Most tall people are used to being in the spotlight or being in the eyesight of other people. Because of that, tall people have a choice. Either they can say, "I don't care what they think. . ." and go about what it is that they do. Or I can say, "If they're going to see me, I might as well give them something good to look at." It is a choice to give others a positive experience. Therefore, that's what I do as a Stand Tall Leader. It doesn't matter if I'm in the grocery store, in the airport, walking down the street, at my son's school as a coach, or even at home. That's something that I keep in mind.

The same thing relates to you as a leader in your school. As the leader, everyone is going to see you no matter what. You're not going to blend in. Playing hide and seek in your school isn't really an option (as much as we do want to do that). Everyone is watching everything that you do and everything that you don't do. Since they are watching everything that you do and everything that you don't do, you might as well give them something good to look at. Reinforce what is important to you in your school. What are those attitudes and behaviors that are relevant that you respect? You need to model that. If you look back to what we talked about earlier as it relates to the results formula, the very first one is respect. What do you respect? What is important to you? You need to emphasize that and show that every time you're in the hallways. Every time you walk out of your office. Every time someone walks into your office. Reinforce those attributes and beliefs consistently. The more that you reinforce those beliefs and those attributes, the more that others will believe that's what we are about here. That's what we do here. Others will start to mimic those behaviors and actions.

So, the next time that you are walking down the hallway and you are on your way to that special class that always has a few issues and your mind is focused on what you're going to say or do when you go in there, and couple of students walks by—take a second to think about what you respect and what is important. Take a moment to showcase what that is either by your body language or how you greet them. How can you emphasize what it is you respect in your daily actions? It means something.

As the leader, everyone is going to see you no matter what. You're not going to blend in. #standtallstatement

It is important to understand, you don't want to be phony and fake. I know some of you who are reading this are probably thinking, well, that's just not my personality to be Mr. or Mrs. Joy. Then I suggest you rethink the position you are in and what it is that you respect. If what you respect is discipline, students being quiet, and being the perfect rule follower, then you need to find a positive way to showcase that in your actions. Notice, I said the word *positive*. Again, a Stand Tall Leader doesn't blend in. Everyone sees everything that you do and don't do, what you say and don't say. Make it a point to reinforce your positive school brand. Every time you pass someone in the hallway, it makes a difference.

Every time you walk past someone in your building or district, you are reinforcing the brand within your school. #standtallstatement

Stand Tall Ideas

CAUGHT

Have you ever looked into a locker of a middle/high school student? It can range from a beautiful space that is organized and color coordinated to a bottomless pit of despair. A great way to transform your locker interiors from drab to fab is to have a CAUGHT program.

Administrators or guidance counselors can walk the hallways in the morning as the students enter the building. This is an ideal opportunity to meet and greet the students and staff. As they walk the hallways, take note of some of the lockers that look great. Stop and talk with a student who has a great locker. Emphasize how the locker is organized and decorated. Don't worry about focusing on lockers that are not organized. Simply focus on the "WOW" lockers. As you talk with the student, be sure to write their name down and give them a "CAUGHT" magnet.

(*Continued*)

Your local merchandise printer can make a "CAUGHT" magnet very easily. If you don't have a local printer, consider printing signs on business card paper and stick magnets on the back. Students love to have magnets in their lockers. Pick some fun exciting lettering and designs. The "CAUGHT" magnet is a great VTW recognition. It is Visible (other students can see it), Tangible (something they can keep and hold on to), and Walk-Aroundable (can be displayed in more than one location).

At the end of each day or week, take the names of the students who were "CAUGHT" and announce their names during your announcements, display them in the hallway, or show them on your internal television station. As the news spreads, you will be surprised how amazing and organized the lockers in your school will be. The end result of the "CAUGHT" program is that students are more organized, newsletters are going home and not ending up in the bottom of lockers, and students have a sense of pride about the school. Students can be "CAUGHT" doing the right thing.

See the Signs

Look around your school. What messages are people seeing? I'm not speaking metaphorically. What are the actual written signs within your school? Many schools have premade banners that you can get from a catalog. I agree, some of the banners are very good and share a quality message. Nevertheless, I feel it to be important to showcase written signs that are specific to the vision, culture, and mission of your school. Additionally, think creatively about where the signs will be displayed.

Creative sign display locations:

- Door windows
- Floors and steps
- Food trays
- Back of chairs
- Mirrors
- Inside every locker
- Parking spots
- Marquee
- School letterhead

Think carefully about what words you will use. Don't use too many quotes or statements. Stick with a few that drive home the mission and vision of the school. Repeat the quotes and statements often. The goal is to purposefully encourage the school community to embrace the vision of the school.

Greeter

When you go to the Disney Store, who do you see standing at the entrance? That's right, a greeter. A greeter is used at the entrance to say hello to everyone and to make them feel good as they enter the store. I took the same concept and used it in the school for morning arrival. Teachers are assigned a location for morning hallway or bus duty. We simply change the name from hallway duty to morning greeter. The focus is to say hello to as many students as possible. You want to make the students feel happy and welcome at the school. We do not know what the students are coming to school with. Sharing a smile and a happy face may make all the difference in the world. This idea is 100 percent free! The greeter is still in charge of ensuring safety, but now with a smile and a high five.

Joke of the Day

Every morning during announcements I say the joke of the day. The joke is usually a goofy riddle that may or may not be funny. In fact, the ones that are not funny are the funniest. After saying the joke, I laugh. Even if it is not funny, I laugh. This is done every day we have morning announcements. After doing this for the first few weeks I knew I was on to something big. I started hearing students repeating the jokes in the hallways. Students would come to me with their own goofy jokes. Parents would share that each night at dinner they would ask what the joke of the day was. I even had substitute teachers excited to come to my school just to hear the joke of the day.

What's the big deal about the joke of the day?

The joke of the day sets the tone for learning throughout the day. It starts everyone on a positive note. Everyone likes a good joke. Everyone likes bad jokes, too. Throughout the day students and staff within the school could reflect back on the joke to give them a little pick me up whenever they need it. The joke of the day is a great icebreaker for family discussion. Instead of parents starting the conversation with, "How was your day?" and the child responding, "it was okay. . ." The conversation starts with, "Tell me the joke of the day!" Instantly, dialog starts and you have a worthwhile conversation.

Eventually, I purchased a mailbox and placed it outside of the main office where students, parents, staff, and community could leave jokes for me. If I said a student's joke during the announcements, they would get recognition and a small prize. Saying the joke of the day takes less than a minute. You do not have to be a good joke teller to do it. It will be even funnier if you don't know how to tell a joke. Below are a few of my favorite jokes. Additionally, my favorite joke book is *Jokelopidia*. This book has a ton of jokes that are categorized into topics.

How does a crazy person get through the forest?
He takes the psychopath!

What did the lightning bug say when he got stepped on?
I'm delighted!

(*Continued*)

Why are pirates so mean?
They just AAAARRRR!

What do you call cheese that doesn't belong to you?
Nacho cheese!

Where does Captain Hook keep his treasure chest?
Under his treasure shirt!

CHAPTER · FOUR
Stand Tall Leaders Value Relationships

4.1. Expectations

I went out to eat at a local restaurant last month. This is not the first time I went to this particular restaurant. I did not think that this experience would be any different than any other. Boy, was I wrong. It started with a horrible parking spot. The hostess did not acknowledge me when I entered and stood right in front of her. Good grief, I'm 6′7″ tall. How can you miss me! The waiter did not get our order quickly and the lemonade was watered down. Overall, the experience was just not good. The experience did not meet my expectations.

All relationships are based on expectations. Whether you meet someone new or have known someone for a while, it really does not matter. You're going to have expectations. I've heard people say that they have no expectations of others. They are wide open and take others as face value. That's not true; there is always that level of expectation. There is always that expectation that you want to have happen and things that you want to see take place. It does not matter what type of relationship is. If it is a marriage, you have expectations that your spouse will not cheat on you. Expectations that you'll spend time together, expectations that you'll listen. If it's a friendship, you expect that they are going to be a loyal friend. Be supportive. Hang out and communicate. Support each other.

Expectations within a school, you have a certain behavior that you are expecting from the students. You expect them to try their best. You expect them to follow instructions and to get along with each other. Within the working environment, you have expectations that others will do their work. Expect that they will support your work and support each other and be cordial. So, no matter what the situation may be, there are always certain types of expectations.

Now, the problem comes into play when we have expectations and either other people do not step up or follow through with those expectations that you have or when others do not step up to that level of expectation. That's when you have some issues, turmoil, and feelings that get hurt. It damages relationships. When people do not fulfill those expectations, that conflict definitely dives into that relationship. When expectations are not met people either respond by lashing out or keeping it in. Neither of them ends well. Overall, people lash out from expectations that are not fulfilled.

It does not look good on the person who lashing out or on the person who does not fulfill the expectation. A lot of times when people lash out, it shows the darker side of who they are and what they really think of others. It damages the relationship even more as well as the person who did not fulfill the expectation. It brings to light that they are not responsible enough to fulfill what the expectation is. The one who is lashing out may be perceived by others as a complainer, petty, or not easy to work with. Therefore, you have to keep an eye on how you go about showcasing those who have not done the expectations that you were hoping for.

Let us look at those who keep it in internally. When others do not do what is expect, it eats away at you, it bothers you, it builds up inside. Trust is reduced. Even if you are at a type of person who thinks, it's not a worry. It does. There is a certain bit of angst that takes place inside. Eventually it's going to come out. It may not come out toward the person that it should come out against. It may come out against others who have nothing to do with the expectation to begin with. You may damage a relationship. You may end up with burnout and other frustrations that get in the way. It goes right back to eventually lashing out anyway. So, in order to improve relationships, you must first understand the types of expectations that can cause conflict. They are the different types of broken expectations.

Once you have a clear understanding of the types of broken expectations, then and only then you can start focusing on what needs to happen in order to fix those broken expectations. There are three types of broken expectations that could cause conflict.

4.1.1. Unvoiced Expectations

An unvoiced expectation is basically a lie. Unspoken expectations mean that you have an expectation of someone else, but it was not voiced to that person. In situations like this, we assume that others know what the expectation is. There are times that you would just assume, is not it obvious? Do you not know this? It's common sense. It's right in front of you. These are all basic things that are stated when an expectation is not voiced, it's a lie unspoken.

You are expecting something, but you never voiced it to make sure that it is clearly understood. As a leader, many times we have expectations of the staff or those who work under us, but yet they do not get it. It's not clearly voiced. The communication is not clear.

When a couple gets married they have to learn how to live together. One day the wife did the laundry. When she was done with the laundry, she took the basket and placed it outside of the laundry room. The husband walked by the laundry room, stepped over the basket, and continued on. She took the basket and moved it to the kitchen. The husband walked into the kitchen, stepped over the basket, and continued on his way. She moved the basket in front of the stairs. As he was going to the stairs, he stepped over the basket and jogged up the stairs. She then she took the basket and placed it on the landing of the stairs, just past four steps. Again, as he was heading upstairs, he went up the few steps, stepped over the basket on the landing, and continued on his way. At that point, the volcano erupted! She blasted her new husband with the many reasons why he should have picked up the basket and taken it upstairs! How could he not have known the expectation? This was an unvoiced expectation.

I know, I know, I know, you are thinking, "Come on, how could he not know what to do?" As a child in the husband's house, whoever did the laundry would carry the baskets upstairs and then each person would grab their own basket to put it away once it was upstairs. When the wife was growing up, whoever did the laundry would place the basket in the hallway and then whoever walked by would grab the baskets and take them upstairs. I'm not saying one is right or one is wrong; both examples have different expectations. If those expectations were voiced there would not have been conflict.

> **An unvoiced expectation is a lie unspoken.**
> **#standtallstatement**

4.1.2. Unrealistic Expectations

An unrealistic expectation means that you are expecting something that is impossible to be fulfilled. This just cannot happen. All of the possibilities and all of the things that could make an outcome take place are not available. There's not enough support. There's not enough understanding. There are not enough people on the team. There's not enough time. There are many of these other factors that are involved with these types of expectations, but it's just unrealistic to be able to fulfill them. When this happens, there is, again, a very clear problem with communication. The viewpoints of either people or either side are skewed. All the necessary information is not provided on both sides. Even if it is clearly understood. Because when you have an unrealistic expectation that is put on someone else, you have the other person feeling a sense of desperation, a sense of unwillingness or inability to have a certain level of respect for the person who's giving that unrealistic expectation.

4.1.3. Unmet Expectations

This third type of expectation that may cause conflict is probably the one that's the most damaging. An unmet expectation means that, one, it is clearly stated and clearly voiced. Two, it is realistic, it makes sense. Three, someone did not step up and do what it is that needed to be done. An unmet expectation can be the most damaging because it shows that there is something missing in all parts of the relationship. Other things may have come into place that has prevented someone from doing what it is they need to do. The other possibility is that they may not care as much about why it needs to get done. The value of what the expectation was for one person was not at the same level as the other person. When someone does not step up and do the expectation that is asked of them, it could have rippling effects. It can cause many other things not to happen or to not take place. So therefore, it is very important that all those within the relationship meet the expectations.

Things will not improve unless you deal with broken expectations. Here's the thing. A lot of times when you have a broken expectation in a school, what happens? We talk about them! You know it's true. We talk about them to our friends, other colleagues, we roll our eyes, we grumble, we sigh deeply. That is not solving anything. It's important that you deal with the broken expectations, whether it's an unvoiced, unreal, or unmet expectation. Ignoring the broken expectations will eat away at you and not resolve the problem. Talking about the person who broke the expectations does not look good on you and does not resolve the problem. So therefore, it must be dealt with so that you can resolve the issue and move on.

All three of the unhealthy expectations are usually birthed out of and connected to previous expectations that might not have been met. Often, there are situations where a previous expectation was unvoiced, unreal, or unmet that may not have anything to do with this specific expectation. But because we don't want to be hurt in the same way as the previous broken experience, we put up barriers or blocks to protect ourselves. But now new people are feeling the wrath of the previous broken expectations. How fair is that? That is why it's important that unmet unvoiced and unrealistic expectations are dealt with.

Things will not improve unless you deal with broken expectations.
#standtallstatement

4.2. How to Move Past Unhealthy Expectations

Now that we understand the three types of unhealthy expectations that can cause conflict, we need to discuss how you get past them. How do you move on? There are four ways to help you really focus on moving past unhealthy expectations.

4.2.1. Go There

You must be willing to go there. And when I say "go there," you have to snap your fingers and roll your neck. Do not be afraid to talk about what the unhealthy expectation was and what happened – no matter how uncomfortable it will be. It's important that it is addressed. If you just ignore it, the other person or people who did not meet the expectation will either think that it's okay or that it wasn't that important. It connects to your integrity, **speaking out for what you believe in**. If you believe that what you expect from others is important, you need to speak up and say something. Go to them. Talk to them about what unhealthy expectation took place and how it was broken. You must be willing to go there to talk about it.

4.2.2. Cut the Apron Strings

You need to cut the apron strings from the problems and the issues of the past. You cannot worry about things in the past that may have led up to this. Focus specifically on the expectation. You have to leave and cleave. Leave the old and cleave to what is the focus here and now. Leave the problems that have led up to the issue. The focus is now. There is no WE until now. Focus on the now. Try not to go back in time to revisit every tiny detail. Say, "This is the expectation that was not addressed, and we need to focus on this right now." Even if the person who broke the expectation keeps focusing on the past, be strong Stand Tall Leader and refocus the conversation back toward now.

4.2.3. Push Through the Pain

It's not going to be easy. It's not going to be fun to address broken expectations. Whenever you address someone about something they did not do, they are going to be either defensive or remorseful and it's going to get uncomfortable. It's going to feel a bit awkward. But you need to push past that. The goal is to come to a common understanding, do not laugh it off and pretend there is not a concern. It may hurt. Things may be said that may hurt your feelings, but the goal is to redirect the focus onto the true issue. Remember, the person who broke the expectation may be defensive at this time. Keep in mind that it's a part of the process. It's a process of talking and discussing the need. It's not one person telling the other person off. It's a process and a discussion.

4.3. Selflessness

You have to choose to be selfless. Remember, it's not always just about you. It's about whatever the situation is. What is it that has been done in your school? What do others need? How do you make this happen? Whatever it takes, do not give up. Try not to make it very personal and focus specifically on what the necessary outcomes are, you CAN move forward. You can try to repair the relationship as it relates to the broken expectations. Just because it's difficult and takes some time does not mean you let it go. Maybe you need to step away for a little bit. Come back and revisit it later. If you take a break, that's fine. Just make sure that you get a clear understanding of the timing, what the expectations are and how to fulfill it.

Look at your school, community, and relationships. Look at what it is that they need. Remember, it's not about you, it's about the needs of the school. It's about the students. It's about the community. It's about the relationship between you and the other person. So, do not be so selfish. Remove yourself from the situation. Think about the expectation as an item that needs to be studied and worked on.

Broken expectations can ruin the culture and climate of a school. Broken expectations can ruin relationships. It can even ruin you as a leader. If you truly want to be a Stand Tall Leader, you have to understand that you need to be clear in what it is that you want for your expectations. You have to be realistic with the type of expectations you ask of others. You have to make sure that expectations are being met and hold people accountable for them. You do this with love, understanding and making sure that you are setting that example by following through the expectations that you have as a Stand Tall Leader. This connects directly to your Integrity (A set of beliefs, values, and actions that others can depend on.). Remember, you cannot play hide and seek. You do not blend in. You're out on display all the time. So therefore, set the example. Fulfill those expectations and hold others to the expectations that you want them to have.

Broken expectations can ruin the culture and climate of a school.
#standtallstatement

Stand Tall Ideas

Monthly Minute

Once a month, provide a video to the staff that reinforces the values and focus of your school. Showcase what you respect. This strengthens your mission, brand, and integrity. Make it a little personal. Don't be so stiff! If people feel like they know you on a personal level, they are more likely to trust you. Just use your cell phone and hold it in front of you. Being less formal makes it come across as more real and relatable. It will appear if you are always thinking about this stuff and you "just had to share."

Paint Party Faculty Meeting

Use one of your faculty meetings to have a paint party. Have the staff paint an image of the school mascot or logo. This bonds the staff together. Hang the paintings within the school so that the students can see. Have the students guess who did what painting as a fun activity.

4.4. The Top Four Ways to Maintain and Attract the Best Substitute Teachers

How do you support your substitutes? Yes, I said substitute teachers. Day in and day out they come to "fill in" for your absent teachers. The way I see it, as building principal, I would want the very best substitutes. Additionally, I never want to be without substitutes. I remember days when

I would be short several substitutes and I had to be creative in order to cover all classes. That rarely happened after changing a few things. After making these slight changes, I have every available substitute running into my school and doing all they can to stay. Here is what I did.

4.4.1. Hello

In the morning as teachers and substitutes arrive to school, I tried to stand by the front counter where the sign-in sheet is. I make it a point to say hello to every substitute who enters the main office. As you know, some substitutes are regulars. They are at the school so often they are like one of the staff. I make sure I greet them with the same excitement as all the other substitutes. A simple hello can mean so much. If there is a new substitute that I have not seen before, I make it a point to shake his/her hand and welcome to him/her to school. If I am able, I will do quick introductions of others in the office who could provide assistance. Often the school secretary does the introductions, but whenever I can, I try.

4.4.2. How Is it Going?

Throughout the day, whenever I see a substitute, I ask, "How is it going?" I'll be honest, sometimes I do not want to know. It would be so much easier to walk by with a smile and a nod. At times, I force myself to ask how they are doing. Most of the time, they say fine. Every now and then, they give me some details about a difficult class. Immediately, I am on the walkie-talkie to get support or walk into the classroom to show my presence. The focus is to provide support and make sure they are appreciated. The same actions and attitude need to be shown by the entire staff at the school. The goal is for the substitute to feel overwhelmingly supported by everyone at the school. On many occasions I have had substitutes say, "This place is amazing! Everyone cares about me!"

4.4.3. Hang Your Hat

There are times when substitutes must travel from room to room. Because of the traveling schedule, they have to carry all of their things with them throughout the day. The other option is to ask one of the classroom teachers to place their things in the classroom and hope the teacher is in the room so they can get their things at the end of the day. What I have done is get a set of portable lockers and place them against the wall in the teacher's lounge. Additionally, I had a coat rack placed in the same room. Substitutes are informed that they are welcome to keep their things in the lockers in the teacher's room and hang their coat/hat on the coat rack. Some of the regular substitutes bring a small lock and key with them in order to secure their materials. Eventually, we got some key locks to give to substitutes to use for the day. This is a very easy action that is hugely appreciated by the substitutes.

4.4.4. Here Is a Shirt

If I have a substitute who is a regular and we can always depend on, I give him/her a staff shirt. This is huge to a substitute. Once I give a substitute a staff shirt, he/she is committed to the school. Also, if a substitute has been to the school at least 25 times, he/she is allowed to be in the staff photo. I know that every time a need for a substitute opens, I am guaranteed to have at least one person who will fill the position and dedicate their mind, body, and soul to the school. As a principal, that is what I want.

Through this simple process I have the most dedicated and competent substitutes available. I have had many substitutes say that they will pick my school over any other school on the roster. They make that commitment because they do not feel invisible and do feel appreciated.

4.5. Retreat!

Every summer when I was a building-level and district-level administrator, the district would pull the administrators from the building for several days to provide professional development and planning. We would call it an administrative retreat. I never really understood why they would call it that. I suppose it was because we would leave or retreat from our buildings in order to reorganize and come forward again with a new plan of action. Kind of like the military. Personally, I think that we should not call it a *retreat* but an administrative *advance*. The goal is not to run away but to move us forward. What we learn and what we do is to move our schools and our district forward. We are advancing the cause. We are advancing our knowledge. We are advancing our schools and district. Therefore, this idea is to simply change the name of the summer administrative training. Do not call it a retreat. Call it an advance.

4.6. Reasons to NOT Recognize

As you know, recognition of students and staff is very important. Recognition of others' actions motivates and empowers them to continue moving in the right direction. Also, as you know, there are those who have a problem with recognition. They do not see the value in it and always have a negative comment or argument about it. When that happens, you may not have the right answer to defend recognition or the right witty comeback ready. That is when you think about it two hours later and then come up with the right response. In an effort to help you have the right response every time, here are the top six reasons to not give recognition, and what to say in response.

1. *I do not know how:* For those educators who say they do not know how to give recognition, the answer is to *Just Ask*. Asking someone how you can recognize them is a form of recognition in itself. "You did a wonderful job. I want to recognize you. What can I do to recognize you?" 99% of the time they will say, "No, do not worry about it." Here's the thing, the act of asking is recognition. You are taking time to take note of what was done. Just ask!
2. *I do not have time:* People always say, "I do not have time for this recognition stuff. Do you know what I have on my plate? Do you know what lesson I have to do? Do you know what my scope and sequence looks like? Do you know what I've got going on in my life?" The question to ask them back is, "Do you have time to whine, cry, moan, and complain about everything else that's going on? It's amazing how you find time to do that, but you do not have time to say, way to go! Good job! You are awesome! Very proud of you!" It takes less than a second to recognize someone for their accomplishments. I'm sure they can find plenty of time to complain, and you can find plenty of time to recognize.
3. *People do not care about it:* The number-one reason people leave a job is because they feel that they are not getting recognized for their efforts. There are tons of studies highlighting that money is not the main reason for someone leaving a job. Money is not the biggest influence for staying at a job and doing your best work. It's always recognition. The same rolls right down to the student level. Students feel like nobody cares if they work hard and do their best. Who cares? Showing recognition and appreciation really makes all the difference in the world.
4. *It's not my job:* Some say, "I come to work, and I teach science. It's not my job to do all this recognition stuff." The question again is, "Is it your job to whine, cry, moan and complain about everything going on in the school? Is it an official part of your job to gripe about what you do not like?" Please let me see your contract. Oh, here it is. Article Four... Line two... *complain about everything*. My bad, please continue on. It does not say in the curriculum or job description that you have to recognize others, but it also does not state that you were supposed to whine, cry, complain, and moan about everything, either, so get to it and recognize others. This statement clearly connects

It does not say in the curriculum or job description that you have to recognize others, but it also does not state that you were supposed to whine, cry, complain, and moan about everything, either, so get to it and recognize others.
#standtallstatement

the difference between compliance and commitment. *Compliance* is coming to work and doing your job. *Commitment* is doing your job and recognizing others to do their best as well.

5. *Why reward people for just doing their job?* I'm sure you have heard many times that it's the students' job to do work and learn. Why go out of your way to recognize them for what they are supposed to do? Say this, next time that you have the big game. You know, the big basketball or football game championship. Everybody is there and the stands are packed. Nobody cheer for the players until the end! Everyone sit silently until the end of the game. At the end of the game, that is when you applaud for the players. "Bravo. Good job. Love what you did in the second quarter. That was excellent." Does that make any sense? NO! Then the question is, why are you cheering for the players? Isn't it their job to play the game? If the football moves forward an inch, people will cheer and go crazy for the players. "Come on! You can do it!" If the football moves backward an inch, people will cheer and go crazy for the players. "It's okay! You got this!" That sounds normal for sports, but in schools students are doing what they are supposed to do. Students are doing their "JOB." Students are supposed to learn and yet we do not cheer them on. When students do well, we aren't saying, "Way to go! You can do it!" When students do not do well, we aren't saying, "It's okay! You got this!" What do we do? We wait until the end of the year to do an awards assembly for the few that got it right along the way. Do not get me wrong, I love a good awards assembly, but throughout the year, how are we recognizing the efforts of all the students as they "do their job"? Are we doing that for teachers as well?

6. *It becomes meaningless if done too much:* I'm sure you can think of the people within the school who say or think this recognition stuff is too much. Every time we turn around, we are recognizing the students and staff for something else. People just need to work and get work done. Do me a favor; the next time you have a group of educators together, ask them to raise their hands if any of them have been recognized too much. I'm confident that none of them will raise their hands. "Please stop telling me how awesome I am." If anyone does raise their hand, they are lying or not deserving of the recognition they are getting.

   As long as the recognition is genuine, I do not see how it could be done too much. Recognition needs to be connected directly to what you respect in your school or district. People within the school need to know what the expectations are and what the recognition system is. That way they are working toward earning the recognition. Far and in between should recognition be a surprise. That is why there are *no surprise rewards.* When people know what the process, expectations, and

> **When people know what the process, expectations, and outcomes are, and they work hard through the process to reach their goal, they deserve to be recognized.**
> **#standtallstatement**

outcomes are, and they work hard through the process to reach their goal, they deserve to be recognized. If they happen to reach that outcome multiple times, then they get recognized multiple times. How dare you NOT recognize them for their efforts! If the process is clear, I do not see how it can be done too much.

Stand Tall Ideas

Start the Morning Statements

When students enter the school, you want them to have a positive mindset and be ready to start the day. This process of starting the day positively can begin the moment the students enter the school. Get a set of positive statement signs that can be held by staff person at morning arrival. Each sign could be a quote or just a word or two. They do not have to be professionally made. You could get some poster paper and colorful markers. Just make sure you think carefully about what you want it to say. Get a set of 10–12 signs. Rotate them every week or every other week. Again, this reinforces what you respect within the school.

Positive Post-It Day

One day a month, use Post-Its to write positive notes to each other throughout the school. Each person gets five notes:

- Two for friends
- Two for staff or others who are not friends
- One for self

Say Students' Names

Locate a student who you do not know. Find the student's name in the yearbook or ask a teacher what the student's name is. Find the kid in the hallway and say his/her name with a positive greeting. If the student asks, "How do you know my name?" Respond by saying, "Are you kidding me, everyone knows you. You are a rock star!"

Teachers Standing Ovation

Think throughout the year when would be the best times for teachers to applaud students. This is a great opportunity for the students to feel empowered and have a sense of either accomplishment or acceptance:

- New student orientation
- First day of school

- Last day of school
- Eight graders visiting school
- First day as seniors
- Last day as seniors
- Graduation
- College acceptance day

GPA Championship

The Team GPA Championship rewards the varsity team with the highest in-season GPA. All of the fall varsity sports compete against each other for the highest First Grading Period GPA. In the spring, varsity teams compete based on Third Grading Period GPA.

Here's how it works: Coaches and captains are reminded of the competition at preseason meetings. Reminders are also sent out at mid-grading period. Coaches are responsible for turning in rosters with GPAs listed by a certain deadline. The athletic director then checks to verify varsity status and GPAs.

Recognition for the highest team GPAs includes:

- Winners are announced via the sports board outside the gym, on morning TV announcements, at the academic or athletic pep rallies and any other appropriate venue.
- Posters with names of winning teams are displayed next to the Team GPA banner in the gym for the entire year.
- Players and coaches receive certificates.
- Coaches receive a framed replica of the team poster.
- Players receive Academic Platinum cards.
- Players receive T-shirts ("Team GPA Champs" is printed on the front, "Victory on the Field and in the Classroom" on the back). If a player is on two or three championship teams in one year, only one T-shirt is awarded and the duplicate winners get free movie passes, etc.
- A letter of congratulations is sent home and copied to the vice principal and guidance counselor for the student's file.
- Championship teams are included in "Athletic Achievement Brochure," which is published and mailed home at the end of the school year.

This is a very competitive program that has made a strong connection between athletics and academics in our school. Not only is this a positive program for the student athletes but will make coaches become more actively involved in their athletes' academic lives.

(*Continued*)

Week of Recognition

Here are ideas that you can implement into your classroom each day for one week. The focus of the ideas is to improve the environment in the classroom and maintain positive relationships with your students. They are easy and quick! Try them out and share with me the tone in the classroom and how the students responded to them. Enjoy!

Monday: High five! Give each student a *high five* as they enter the room. Everyone knows what a high five is. It takes the general basic hello and makes it more exciting. Also, doing this as the students enter the room sets the tone for your time together. Some classrooms even allow students to come up with unique greetings as they enter the class! The atmosphere is upbeat and positive. This may be a shock to your students if you do not usually greet your students as they enter. Try it out!

(Make sure you have a bottle of hand sanitizer close by after touching hands, elbows, or fist bumps with so many kids. Be aware of children who are not fans of touching, and honor their greeting preference.)

Tuesday: Share a story. Think of a positive story you were involved in when you were a child and share it with the class. It does not have to be a super motivational story. It just has to be about you. Your students are very interested in who you are and who you were. Making connections with your students is important. This is an opportunity to let them see the nonteacher side of you. Be careful not to get sucked into a full class discussion about childhood events. You do not need a smooth segue to blend into the lesson. Just share the story and move on to the lesson.

Wednesday: Ask a question. At the start of class, tell the students you will give an award to the student who asks the best question for the lesson. The award does not have to be elaborate. It can be a paper ribbon if you want. The focus is to recognize the educational efforts of the students in the class and stretch their thinking. As each student asks a question, make sure you acknowledge the question and prompt others to "up the ante." Also, make sure you have a great lesson for the students to ask questions. Do not do this if you are planning to review simple math facts. Try the intro to a new subject or review before a test.

Thursday: Shake a hand. As the students leave the class, shake each one's hand. Thank them for their efforts during the class. Make sure you do it right. Give a firm handshake, look in the eyes, and speak clearly. True, some students will think it is weird. Some students would appreciate the gesture. It gives a positive closure to the lesson and your time together. Make sure you have a bottle of hand sanitizer close by after touching hands with so many kids.

Friday: Quote. Write a motivational quote on the board before the students enter the room. Make sure the quote is written big enough on the board for everyone to see. Take a minute or two and discuss the meaning of the quote. Do not turn it into a lesson. Just talk about the quote and give the students time to talk about it. Be careful not to get sucked into a full-class discussion about the quote that prevents your lesson from being taught. The point is to set the tone for the lesson and establish the direction for the day.

4.7. I Just Cannot Help You

As a Stand Tall Leader, your ultimate goal is to help, influence, and develop positive relationships with people. You always have good intentions, but when you want to help, influence, and develop positive relationships with people, you will come across those who just cannot accept the help or do not want the help. They cannot understand the help that you are offering them. Everyone deals with this at some level. If you have teenagers or have worked with teenagers, I am sure you have experienced this. I can see you shaking your head yes right now. How many times have experienced this from a teenager? After you have provided guidance, direction, and assistance, they are hardheaded and have to learn the hard way? You are so frustrated and dumbfounded as to why the teenager is taking the hardest road to get to the results, they think they are going to get it instead of just listening and accepting the help provided?

As a leader within your school or district what happens is you end up getting frustrated or you end up changing your focus, vision, or practice in order to accommodate these one, two, or three people. This can cause turmoil in your leadership and the organization. Okay, okay, maybe you do not change for those who will not change, but at least it is on your mind; weighing you down and causing you to second guess your actions. You know it is! Even if you put forth a good face in front of everyone else, it still bothers you.

As a Stand Tall Leader, your ultimate goal is to help, influence, and develop positive relationships with people. #standtallstatement

Please understand that most of the time when others do not accept help it's not because of you as the leader, it's them. You can continue to focus on what is most important and move the ship forward, or you can continue to focus all of your efforts on these few people who will move you away from your goals. In order to prevent that from happening, you need to understand the type of people who you just cannot help. By understanding these people, it will help you better lead everyone else and also understand where they stand with resistance.

4.7.1. You Cannot Help People Who Do Not Think They Need It

It's hard to help someone who thinks that they do not need any help at all. What you end up doing is spending most of your time trying to convince the person that they need the help to begin with. But if they do not think they need any help and they are fine with the way they are, they will continue the way they are. It is the steepest continual uphill battle. Think through your experience as an educator. I am sure you can identify a few others who clearly needed help, but they had no clue that they needed it. Somehow, they developed a reality within their mind that established them as the expert, and everything they do is just fine.

These people do not want help, and your efforts to help them are going to result in a power struggle. Remember, they already think they are, "the expert and everything they do is just fine." They are going to talk about you to others. They are going to twist the truth. They are going to change the outcome of what it is that you are trying to do and possibly sabotage what needs to be done. They do not want any help. They do not think they need it. They do not see how they need it. They do not see the bigger picture.

What can you do with these people? You can continue on without them. You could try to show them what the reality is around them, but think about this. That is just going to end up making you focus on different areas and taking you away from the ultimate goal of what it is that you need to do as a leader. Keep an eye out for them to make sure they are not causing any damage or sabotaging the outcome for others. If that is the case and you are their direct supervisor, you may need to use your authority to mandate specific actions through an improvement plan or directive. For this type of person, you need to operate with the compliance realm. This person is not going to give you the commitment that you are trying to develop and foster within the rest of your followers. Even though you cannot help those who do not think they need it, as the leader you can insist that they move in the appropriate direction of compliance in order to prevent damage.

You cannot help those who do not think they need it, but as the leader, you can insist that they move in the appropriate direction of compliance in order to prevent damage.
#standtallstatement

4.7.2. You Cannot Help People Who Know They Need It and Do Not Want It

You know these people; they know that they are not doing as well as they could be. They know that they could do better. They know that they want to be better at what it is that needs to be done, but their pride gets in the way. I am sure you have come across these people. Usually, you find out that they know they need help but are unwilling to take it from someone else. A sympathetic friend of the person who needs help realizes that he/she is sinking and has confided in a friend. That friend is torn about letting you know and wants the best for the struggling friend and does not know what else to do. Sound familiar?

These people just will not let their pride come down or humble themselves enough in order to receive help. In many cases, these people will go from person to person, picking small bits of information and piecing their actions together in order to try to improve. They feel the pressure to change. They will spend a great deal of energy avoiding you just to prove that they can do it on their own.

All you can do for them is to offer the help for them, outline the criteria and the expectations of what it is that they need to have done and the amount of time. If they do not do it, they have to unfortunately suffer those consequences. This person has the commitment but does not know how and is unwilling to ask how to become compliant. They have to come to the realization on their own that they must ask for the help. There's not much you can do about it. They know that the help is there. They have to get over that threshold on their own. At times, you may be able to work with the sympathetic friend to provide some guidance, but that is not always a solid plan. All you can do is lay it out there for them, and hopefully they'll end up coming around to be able to accept the help.

4.7.3. You Cannot Help People Who Do Not Want It

The cost of not changing has not cost them enough. Unfortunately, you may need to wait for a crisis to take place in order for them to understand that they need help. These people do not want the help, similar to the first ones. They not only think they do not need the help; they just do not want it. The only way that they are going to be able to see that they need the help is when something bad happens. Usually, you can see the crisis coming a mile away. You have had the one-on-one conversations. You have had the mandated improvement plan. You have had others talk to him/her. You have even prayed about it. Regardless of it all, this joker just will not accept the help.

When the crisis takes place (and it will), these people will do one of two different things. One, they will be in panic mode, which usually ends up making things worse. They will scramble around, hiding behind you as the leader to try to fix it. They will pull in other people; they will attempt to hide things. It will always come out in the end that they made a huge mistake. Even if they are able to hide it at first, it always comes out! The worst part about it is that you as the leader will usually have to fix it or take the heat for their problem and unwillingness to get the help needed.

Two, they will run to you right away and asked you to fix the big huge mess up that they made. Hopefully, at that point they will be able to understand that they do need help. Sometimes these crises are damaging to their job and even their life. Hopefully, it's not damaging to the students that they are serving. Unfortunately, those are the times when the help is going to be offered to them and they'll actually take it.

Sadly, these people may never have commitment and will continually struggle with compliance. As a leader, you may need to make the decision to either keep them or let them go if you can.

4.7.4. You Cannot Help People Who Do Not Want It from You

Sometimes it IS you. For whatever reason, you are the one who they just cannot get over to accept the help. You know those people that just do not like you, no matter what offer you are giving them. It does not matter what help you are giving. It does not matter how you set things up for them, they just do not like you. It might be your personality; it might be the position that you hold; it might be because they had a bad experience with the person who was in the position before you. So now they are transferring that anger or resentment onto you. Because it's you, they just will not accept any help. They just do not like whatever it is that you are doing. And again, they may just sabotage whatever needs to be done. You have to get to the point of being okay for them to get help from somewhere else. It does not have to be you.

This is where you are looking for your support group and you are looking at their support group. You need to look wherever you can to provide assistance for them. Be careful! At times, if they realize that you are the one who is fostering the help and support through other avenues, they will continue to put up walls of resistance.

For those who are in leadership in a school building, recognize that some teachers and staff might not accept a new idea or new concept from you *because* it came from the leader. These are the times and the situations where you need to find the educators or staff members that you can trust. See if it's possible for them to provide assistance and make it better for the rest of your staff or those around you.

Also, this is an opportunity where you can use a committee. In a committee, you can post something and then the committee can move it forward and hopefully make it work in a direction that's best to help those who need it. As you know, sometimes people see leadership positions in a certain light, regardless of what it is that you have done as a leader. Therefore, it may be very difficult to be able to help those who have the narrow view of leadership.

Sometimes people see leadership positions in a certain light regardless of what you have done as a leader. #standtallstatement

4.7.5. You Cannot Help People Who Are Unwilling to Do What It Takes to Get It Done

You want to help people and give them all the tools that they need. They may agree with what it is that you are saying. They may even agree with the process. They may agree with the outcomes in the end. They're just unwilling to step up and do what is necessary to get the job done. You cannot help these people. They do not have the wherewithal. They do not have the stamina. They do not have the grit to step up to get it done. These people might need additional training in order to build that stamina. You need to build the skills so that ultimately you can get to the level that allows them to follow through with a task. This takes time. It is not something that happens quickly, so therefore you may need to step back to build the longevity and perseverance skill set of those around you so that, in time, they can get to the point where they can do what it takes to get it done.

These are the people that may need the continual positive reinforcement and evidence that their efforts produce positive outcomes. I know, I know, you would rather toss them out the fifth story window, but you just cannot do that. This person has the commitment and understands the compliance. They are just too lazy to make either one a true reality. I am sure you have witnessed those who have the "It's good enough" mentality. In that case, they are unable to see your vision. They do not see the value and the personal benefit of doing what it takes to get it done. If they are unwilling to get it done, you just cannot help them now. You will have to help them later.

Thinking back over the five different types of people that you just cannot help, I'm sure you can identify certain staff members and people in your life that fit within each one of these. Maybe there is somebody who fits every single one of them. Now think about how much time and effort you have put into trying to help these specific people. Is it worth it? What was the outcome? Was it stressful? Did they actually get the help that they need? These are all the things that you consider, and you think about when you are the leader. The goal is to make sure that you are focusing on the people and the things within the vision that are going to make the outcomes that you need. With all these different types of people that you just cannot help, you may have to work around them. You may have to just focus on those areas that you can work with. You have to work heavily within maintaining compliance. Maybe you need to build them up to a point that eventually they'll start taking hold and accepting the help from somewhere. But spinning your wheels and continuing your efforts in areas of people that you just cannot help will not benefit you as a leader and grow your organization to the level that it needs to be.

Developing positive relationships is extremely important as a Stand Tall Leader. Take the time to pour into people your love and knowledge. The value of service and deep desire to help is what will strengthen your connections with those you lead. With that said, it is important that you keep in mind what roadblocks can knock you off course when developing the positive relationships and strong climate and culture within your school:

- Have clear expectations that are connected to what you respect. Understand how to repair the relationship when those expectations are broken.
- Recognize others when they do well and earn the rewards that are connected to what you respect; this will build strong relationships. Know what to say to those who believe that recognition is not valuable to the success of the school and individuals.
- Provide help and assistance to those you lead so that they can achieve their goals and get the results you know they can get. Be aware of those who just will not accept the help and have a plan for what to do with them.

Stand Tall Ideas

Cafeteria Staff

How often do you recognize your cafeteria staff? Yes, they are a part of the school family as well. It does not matter if your food services are contracted out. They matter. Each month, take a photo of a cafeteria worker and post it on a board. Ask some questions about the cafeteria staff to get interesting information to hang with the photos. Make sure you highlight the posting during your announcements so that the school family will take notice. It is a small gesture that will go a long way.

- Highlight the cafeteria workers in your parent newsletter or school newspaper.
- Have a bulletin board with the names and faces of all workers.
- Give them a staff T-shirt.
- Remember to let them know when special events take place.
- Always invite them to faculty meetings (even if you know they will not go).
- Include them in staff appreciation activities.
- Encourage thank-you letters from students and staff.
- Place thank-you notes in the kitchen the night before, so they see them when they come in the next day.
- Secretly tell the students that it is national smile at a cafeteria worker day. Do it all day and see how much they notice.

Custodial Staff

Every afternoon everyone leaves the school and the hallways and classrooms are empty. Then something amazing happens. A very dedicated and focused group of unsung heroes appear in the school and start the tedious job of cleaning the building. That's right, I'm talking about your custodial staff.

One of the most important groups within your school is the custodial and maintenance staff. It does not matter if they are members of the district or contracted to an outside company. They are very important to the cleanliness and safety of the school. The school would not run if it were not for them. I am sure there are plenty of horror stories regarding how some of the rooms and hallways appear. Nevertheless, just imagine how it would look if nothing was ever done.

What I have done in my building to recognize the custodial staff is to simply post a sign in the hallway that states, "The cleanliness of this wing is maintained by:" This one simple gesture changes everything. Once you post this sign in the hallway, you are allowing the custodians to show pride in their work. Now everyone knows who keeps this hallway clean. For the hallways that are not so clean, this puts a name to the not-so-clean hallway. I assure you; things will start looking better once a name goes up. If you want to take it to the next level, get a photo of the custodial staff and place it with the sign. Now, a name and a face are attached to the hallway.

When I posted the signs, each of the custodial staff came to me to say "Thank you!" and "Good idea! The director of grounds, business director, assistant superintendent, and superintendent all appreciated the signs. Take the time; say thank you to your custodial and maintenance staff.

Attendance Ice Cream and Dance

An ice cream truck comes to the school on a Friday. The students with perfect attendance for the week get to bring a dollar and buy ice cream. Also have a hallway dance for good grades. Class with the best attendance for the week gets to pick out two or three songs to be played over the intercom and all the students with perfect attendance for the week go out into the hallway by their classroom and dance. They love it.

Lip Sync Battle

Pick a date and time that would work within your schedule. Bring the students together to see and have a full-throttle Lip Sync Battle between students and staff. If it is a surprise to the students, it would be even better. If it is a bigger event, have a surprise one-on-one battle during each of the lunch periods to build excitement.

Free Hugs Friday

Everyone loves Friday. It does not matter if you work in a school or corporate office. Also, lots of people love hugs. Blend them together. Pick one or two Fridays a month as official Free Hug Friday. Then you should know what to do next. Give out as many free hugs as possible. Make sure you enforce the personal space rules, but do not let that stop you. Make sure everyone joins in; teachers, students, staff, and visitors. (Yes, this is just like High Five Friday, duh.)

CHAPTER · FIVE
Stand Tall Leaders Make Strategic, Smart, and Creative Decisions

5.1. What Is Climate and Culture?

What is *climate* and *culture*? School leaders talk about climate and culture all the time. The words *climate* and *culture* are said synonymously without thought. People think that they understand what climate and culture is, but I believe they may not have a deeper understanding of it. Just because people within a school have a bad attitude about the work they do, or students don't participate in activities, you think it is a bad climate and culture. Just because the students chant the school theme during sporting events you think it is a good climate and culture.

Climate and culture are two separate things that feed off of each other and can be controlled. It is very possible to change them through strategic actions and planning over time. But before you can make the change in climate and culture, you need to understand each of them. Once you have the understanding, you can then realize how to start the process of altering them toward what you *respect* and *value*. The following diagram outlines specifically what climate and culture is and how it can be changed.

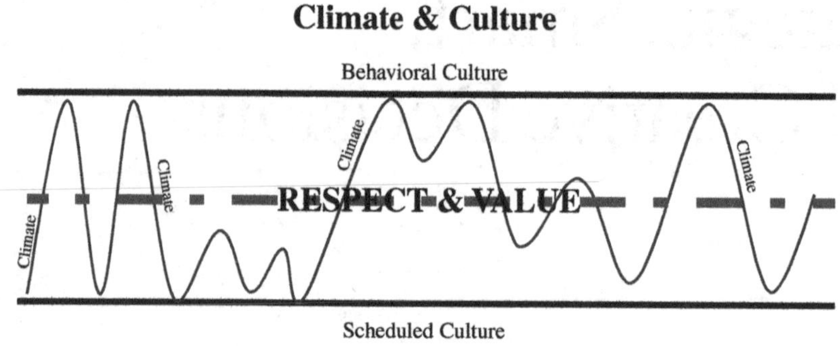

5.2. Respect and Value

We have investigated the importance of identifying what it is you *respect* and *value* within the school. What you respect and value within the school needs to be clearly stated and understood by everyone. That does not always happen. Many schools have mission statements or vision statements. These statements are supposed to ground everyone around a common understanding of what is expected and held as the standard within the school or district. Question: How many can actually recite the mission or vision statement? Who knows what it is? Who knows what it means? Don't get me wrong, I believe that you must have a vision or mission statement that clearly states what you respect and value. A vision or mission statement can do that. You just need to make sure it directly connects with what you respect and value.

What you respect and value within the school needs to be clearly stated and understood by everyone.
#standtallstatement

Within the above chart, what you respect and value within the school is represented by the center dashed line. It is placed in the center because that is what should be at the center of all actions and decisions. It should be the grounding base of the schools culture and climate.

5.3. Climate

The climate is what you feel when you are in the school day to day. What is the feeling in the school when you enter the front doors? How do you feel throughout your day? The climate can change from day to day. The feel of the building on the first day is different than the feel of the building before state testing. The feel of the building before winter break is different than the feel on a random day of March 16. I'm sure you would agree that the feel in the building is very real and can be physically felt by every person inside.

The climate can change from hour to hour within a day. How do you feel when you get to school in the morning? How do you feel just after lunch? The feel of the building right after the students enter the building is different than the feel in the building after a physical education class. Have you ever been in a school when a rumor of a fight spreads through the building? The climate changes very quickly and drastically. Have you ever been in a school when an announcement has been made about the teacher of the year? The climate changes.

Within the above chart, the climate is identified by the wavy line. The line shows that the climate fluctuates continuously. The climate can be high, and it can be low. At times it can be close to what you respect and value and at times it is nowhere near it.

5.4. Culture

Culture is a fancy word for traditions. Traditions is defined as an inherited, established, or customary pattern of thought, action, or behavior. Therefore, the school culture is made up of actions and behaviors of people within the school that happen over and over again. These are the events and behaviors of people that you can expect to happen. And they do happen.

There are two types of culture within a school, *scheduled culture* and *behavioral culture.*

The scheduled culture includes the scheduled events that take place within the school on a yearly, monthly, and daily basis. These events are planned out ahead of time or they are so frequent that it is expected that it will just happen. For example:

- Daily announcements
- Instructional periods of the day
- Graduation
- Rallies
- Grade distribution
- Discipline referrals
- Walking to class every day
- Recognition events

Basically, any scheduled event that takes place that happens on a consistent basis. The scheduled culture are those specific events and how it is handled. How are daily announcements done? How does grade distribution take place? How are discipline referrals handled? How are students recognized? That "HOW" makes up the scheduled culture.

Scheduled culture includes the scheduled events that take place within the school on a yearly, monthly, and daily basis.
#standtallstatement

Within the above chart scheduled culture is identified as the bottom horizontal line. This line is a solid line because it is repetitive and can anchor a school.

Behavioral culture is what people are saying on a yearly, monthly, and mostly daily basis. Everyone has an opinion about what happens in the school. People experience a variety of events within a school.

- What are people saying about the specific scheduled culture events and actions?
- How are teachers talking to students?
- How are students talking to teachers?
- How are administrators talking to teachers?
- How are people expressing themselves?
- How are people greeted when they visit the school?

- What is tolerated, and what do people say about it?
- What is not tolerated, and what do people say about it?

Basically, it is what is being said over and over again within the school that makes up the behavioral culture. It comes down to how people treat each other on a regular basis. Are people friendly? Are people rude? Are people divisive? Are people compassionate?

Behavioral culture is what people are saying on a yearly, monthly, and mostly daily basis.
#standtallstatement

Within the chart, behavioral culture is identified as the top horizontal line. This line is a solid line because it runs parallel with the scheduled culture.

Scheduled culture and behavioral culture are parallel because they both frame and affect the climate within a school. How people behave and how events take place can alter how people feel from day to day, week to week, month to month and year to year. Think about it. . . If you have a school assembly that was not scheduled well *(scheduled culture)*, students were rushed into the assembly *(scheduled culture)* teachers barked at the students assuming they would not behave *(behavioral culture)* and the administrator put everyone down *(behavioral culture)*, and teachers stood on the sides like guards *(scheduled culture and behavioral culture)*, what would the climate feel like?

The more negative the behavioral culture and scheduled culture are, the further away the line moves from the center. Remember, the center is what you respect and value. The further away those lines move, the worse and more fluctuating the climate becomes. This is why you have schools that have a poor climate and culture. With some schools, you can walk in the front door and feel the poor climate right away. It is just horrible. The longer the behavioral and scheduled culture is allowed to progress negatively, the harder it will become to believe and justify what you say it is you respect and value. This is when you get the statement of a toxic school environment.

What can you do about it? The key is to focus on the center line. The center line is what you respect and value. Many schools say they respect and value one thing, but the regular behaviors and scheduled actions are don't reflect that. This is where the *results formula* comes into play. You must look closely at the actions and events that are carried out within the school on a regular basis. Do they truly align with what you respect and value? Do you get the outcomes that you want to have happen? What actions are being done that are basically spinning your wheels and not having any real impact to move you toward highlighting what you respect and value? If your actions and events are not aligned to what you respect and value, start the *results formula process* and start the change.

Stop and listen! Listen to what people are saying and how they are saying it. Is what they are saying said in a positive way? Are people saying the negative things in a daytime DJ voice? Are people saying positive things with a nighttime DJ voice? What about you? How are you saying things? Remember, as a Stand Tall Leader you don't blend in and everyone sees and hears everything you do and say. Do your actions align with what the school respects and values? Are your actions of high integrity? Do you keep your promises? Do you speak out for what is important? Do you err on the side of fairness? Do you do what you say you are going to do? If people are not speaking and behaving in a way that is not aligned to what you respect and value, step up, be the Stand Tall Leader and start holding people accountable for their actions. Be the example. Start the *results formula* process and emphasize recognizing others when they do what it is that you respect.

This will take time! Stay consistent with the process. Wrap your actions around the results formula. Eventually, people will move from *compliance* to *commitment*. The actions and events will start to change for the better. Reinforce what it is you want to have happen. Do it again and again and again. You will become more established as a Stand Tall Leader and your culture will start moving toward the center of what you respect and value and your climate will become more consistent and in alignment with what you respect and value most.

Stand Tall Action

Write out specifically what you respect and value.

Take an assessment of all scheduled activities and events within your school.

Ask the hard question. . . Does each of these events align with what you respect and value?

If the answer is no to any activity or event, either stop it or change it.

Stand Tall Ideas

B44

As building principal, I felt it was my duty to connect, train, and guide my newer nontenured teachers. It would be irresponsible of me not to share my vision and goals with them and purposefully position them for success. With that in mind, I created the B44 group within my school.

B44 stands for *before four years.* All teachers who have taught in Hartford School for less than four years are welcome to join. We meet once a month in one of the teacher's classrooms. This group is completely voluntary. B44 is separate from the new teacher training series within the district. The goal of B44 is to allow time for the nontenured teachers to have access to me and building administration. During this time, I will share with them my vision of education and the school. It is a very open environment. The discussion flows both ways. During our time together we discuss articles, look at videos, answer questions, explain decisions made, introduce key people in the district, and anything else that may come up. We don't necessarily talk about lesson plans, curriculum, and specific assessment strategies. It mostly revolves around the vision, goals, and what makes the school, the school.

Think of it this way: Hopefully, the new teachers will stay in your school for many years. Why not take the time at the start of their career to develop the strong personal bond? Don't leave it up to chance. As the years go by, you continually strengthen the relationships with your new staff. Ten to 15 years down the line, you will have a very strong staff that understands the vision and will have powerful, positive relationships with administration.

Bulletin Board Upgrade

Most schools have bulletin boards. It is usually up to the principal to determine who decorates what bulletin board when. The concern comes when the boards look bad. Sure, anyone can put some kids' work on a board and call it decorated. Nobody stops to look at it and it does not add to the environment of the school. Here are some ideas to take your boring bulletin boards to the next level:

Theme: Pick a theme for the boards throughout the building for the year or each month. This will allow for a common message to be thread throughout the building.

Color theme: Each month have a color that will be common for all boards.

Where is Waldo: Require that a small school mascot be placed on one or two boards. Encourage the students to find it.

Beyond the frame: Don't just decorate within the frame of the board. Extend the decoration beyond the frame to bring interest to the board.

Directional signs: Place directional signs throughout the building pointing to the board.

Coalition: Have questions posted on one board and answers on another board in the building.

Coming soon: Decorate the board, then cover it with large paper with a "Coming Soon" sign to build anticipation.

Social media: Take photos of the boards in the building and post one a week on the school Facebook or other social media page.

Social media: Post questions on your website or social media sites and provide the answer on a board in the building. This pulls people into the building to get the answer.

Quotes: Provide a bank of positive quotes as a springboard to the decoration of the board.

Name: Name each board a word of character. Whoever is assigned that board must uphold that name with the decoration.

Art teacher: Have your art teacher review the elements of good composition at the start of the school year to set the expectation for bulletin board design.

5.5. Decisions

Within one day we make thousands of decisions. The decision can range from what shirt to wear to what is the best instructional process for a student with an individualized education program (IEP). Decisions you make as a leader are at many different levels throughout the day. In most cases, leaders are on autopilot with decisions. After some time, you get used to thinking things through quickly and giving a decision or process. At times, leaders ponder over the best way to present the decision or what process is needed in order to get the best outcome. Many times, a leader needs to think about who else should be a part of the decision process – or when it should be delegated. Understanding the types of decisions there are and when to let others into the decision-making process will determine the level of success of the decision. But, how often do we as leaders really think about the decisions we make and what level they are used? Also, how often do we tell others about the types of decisions we make and why we make those decisions?

What follows are the *five levels of decision-making.* These five levels break down the types of decisions that are made, who is involved in the decision made, and who is responsible for the decision made. This concept of the five levels of decision-making isn't something new. It has been used within business and corporate organizations. The way that it is described is for the Stand Tall Educational Leader. This is something that can directly impact and influence educational leaders immediately.

5.5.1. Level 1 Decision: No Input from Others

This level is usually reserved for emergency situations. Something has happened that was unexpected, and a quick answer is needed. Usually you are the one who has most of the information or knowledge to make a sensible and clear decision. Follow-up is usually reserved to you and the weight of the responsibility is yours.

This is the level that most school leaders live in. They use Level 1 decision because it is quick and efficient. Leaders feel that Level 1 establishes them as a leader and build the respect of others. Yes, that is true to a point. Just think about how you would feel if every time you go to your superior with a concern and they quickly give an answer and decision every time. You would think they were not listening or never considered your possible solution. Also, how are you building the decision-making ability of others if you are the one always making the decisions? Don't get me wrong, there is nothing wrong with Level 1 decisions, just make sure that it isn't the only way you are making decisions.

5.5.2. Level 2 Decision: Decide after Others' Input

This level allows others on the team to contribute to the solution. It is clearly stated or understood that you are the one making the decision. The decision may be part of the input from others or may not. Follow up is reserved to you, but it is important that you inform others providing input about your decision and thank them for their time.

This level allows the leader to make better informed decisions and start the process of empowering others. How often have you heard others say, "She didn't even ask my opinion!" or "I said what I thought, but he did what he wanted anyway!" This level eliminates that. By clearly stating that you want others input, but you reserve the right to either use their input or not is huge. It sets the ground rules up front. The most important part is giving follow up and thanking others for their time and input. Others will appreciate that you took the time to consider their opinion. Now others say, "At least she asked my opinion," or "I told him what I thought, but I know he may or may not use it."

5.5.3. Level 3 Decision: We Decide Together

This is true collaboration. The level of urgency is not as high and there is time to think things through. This level of decision-making is when voting may be useful. The main focus is that everyone or both of you agrees to move forward or at least to move forward and agree not to sabotage the decision made. Follow up can be delegated to those on the team and communication is vital to the success of the decision made. Within this level you are empowering others within the group, and you have more buy in with the overall process and outcomes.

Fist to Five:

One process that I love is using *Fist to Five* to get understanding and consensus from the group. With this you go through the normal process of discussing and planning out the project or event. When the time comes for the vote, everyone raises their hand with a number from 0–5. Each number indicates what level of acceptance they have to the expected actions and outcomes.

- 5 = I am all in and I LOVE IT! I will even help spread the good word.
- 4 = I am all in and I'll support it.
- 3 = I am in, but I have some reservations about it. I still think it's a good idea.
- 2 = I have some issues with it. I think it has merit, but we need to discuss it more before I say I'm in.
- 1 = This is not a good idea. We need to talk over many parts of this and come to a new outcome.
- 0 = I hate this and will punch you if you do it!

5.5.4. Level 4 Decision: Let You Make the Decision after My Input

At this level you give the control over to someone else or the team. You are a major contributor before decisions are made. You have experience or knowledge that will help in the decision process. What is most important is that you agree with whatever decision is decided by the other person or team. It is up to the other person or team to have follow-up. Make sure you are included in all communication, so you are not surprised with outcomes.

This level of decision-making strengthens the team. Many times, this can be used when the leader has a mentee that has been groomed and is ready to step up. Also, when there are team leaders, department heads, and assistants this level happens automatically. Leaders can get stuck in this level and find it hard to get out. This happens when others keep coming to the leader to get their input first continually. This can be very disruptive and frustrating to the leader who is trying to let go of the reigns. This shows evidence that the person who is now allowed to take the lead either isn't ready or needs an additional push to fly.

5.5.5. Level 5 Decision: You Make the Decision Without My Input

At this level, others are fully empowered. Others know your expectations and vision. They have worked with you enough to know how you would respond and your level of accomplishment. You give trust to others. Follow-up is completely in the hands of those making the decision. You may be involved with the communication or you may not.

It can be difficult determining what level of decision-making you should employ. The most important part in making the decision is to make a decision.

Now here is the magic in using the five levels of decision-making. Let everyone within your school or organization know about the five levels. Then use the five levels when announcing or presenting new situations to them. Simply tell them. By letting everyone else know about what level of decision-making you are using you are preventing the questioning about how decisions are being made. Now, obviously, you would not announce level 1. But level 2–5 are free to use continuously. Just think about it and consider this situation:

You are planning to implement a new program into the school. You send your Friday focus email and let everyone know that a program is in the planning stages. Let everyone know that it will be a level 2 and a voluntary meeting will take place after school. Instantly, everyone knows where their position is as it relates to the decision made. They understand that they can give you their thoughts and opinions, but the final decision is yours.

Let's say you have to plan out a new student recognition, and it needs to be accepted by everyone. You announce to the staff that there is a meeting next week to discuss the new recognition focus and it will be a level 3. Again, instantly everyone knows what to expect going into the meeting. They know they have an equal voice to how it will take place.

The power of the levels of decision-making takes place when you share the levels with everyone, use them and stick to it. It prevents people from saying, "I gave her my suggestion, but as usual she doesn't listen to me. . ." or "I don't know when he wants my input and when he doesn't," or "I never know when I can just go and make it happen or wait for permission." Sharing the levels of decision-making with everyone clarifies how decisions are made and where they stand.

Keep in mind, you are still the leader. If you implemented a level 4, but realized that it is a hot mess you can have a meeting and move it back to a level 3 or 2. All you have to say is why it is a hot mess and state the new level. It would be much easier to swallow that change when they know the parameters of decision-making.

The most important part in making the decision is to make a decision.
#standtallstatements

Stand Tall Ideas

Positive Office Referral

When a student misbehaves, he/she is written up on an office referral form, which has been designed to provide clarification to the office of what the infraction was. There are categories that determine how serious of an action it was and guidance on how to handle it. Usually only students getting in trouble are called to the office. With a positive office referral, staff can write up any student for doing the right thing. The positive office referral form categorizes good behavior so the office can understand what was done. I asked the teachers to send at least one positive office referral a month, but most did two or three. The office administrator would always call down the student and ask him/her if he/she knew why he/she was there? Most of the time, they had no idea and were on the verge of crying. The administrator would read the positive referral and praise the student for his or her actions. It is important to call the student's parent while the student is in the office, then share the news with the parent and pass the phone to the student so they can talk. On many occasions, everyone in the room and on the phone was in tears. During the recognition rally, all the students who received positive office referrals were recognized again.

Musical Photos

Most schools have a winter and spring concert. The students sing, dance, and perform for parents, family, and friends. The night performances are the best! With over 18 years watching performances

(*Continued*)

as an educator, as well as performing in them since grade school, I've seen a lot. This is usually what happens:

The student performers enter the stage getting ready to perform.

Parents stand up and start to wave at their children.

The children can't see them, so the parents start to yell names.

Parents start taking photos from their seats.

Some of the more aggressive parents move toward the stage.

Some bend down as they walk thinking they cannot be seen.

Once near the stage or in the aisle they start calling for their child to look.

Usually, the parent is very tall and blocks everyone.

Once the concert starts, some parents stay in the aisle or set up a tripod in front of everyone.

You are lucky if a fight does not break out in the crowd.

Does this sound like your concerts? I decided to prevent this from happening at the concerts by allowing three to four minutes for parents to come forward and take photos. The first time I got on the microphone and announced that we would take a couple minutes for photos, you would have thought I just given everyone a pound of gold. Parents instantly moved toward the front, waved, called names, and took a bunch of photos without worry. As each minute passed by, I announced, ". . .two minutes left for photos." At the end, everyone respectfully returned to their seats and the concert started.

As each new performance group entered the stage, I allowed time for parents to take photos. Yes, the concert was 15 minutes longer. So what? The end result was photos and memories that will last forever.

An additional photo opportunity I started this year was to set up a display in the foyer of the school. I informed the parents that at the end of the performance they could take photos in front of the display in the foyer. I was shocked at how many parents had their children pose with instruments, friends, and me! It made for a wonderful school event.

PS: Make sure you tell the students that there will be three to four minutes of photos before they perform. Instruct them to look for their parents, smile, and don't complain.

Welcome Wagon

How are new students welcomed to your school? In most cases, new students get to see the person who registers them in the guidance office, then are given a schedule, walked down to a room, and left to fend for themselves. As the year progresses, those new students may or may not connect with the school community.

When a student leaves a school, what is the process for the student to feel recognized and remembered? The student leaving may have been with the district and fellow peers for many years and have deep connections with other students. When the student leaves, he/she just wants someone to recognize the time they spent at school and be sent off with smiles.

New Students

When a new student registers at the school during the school year, it is an opportunity for the school to truly welcome the new student into the fold. Prepare a large envelope with an image of a wagon on the front and the words "Welcome Wagon." Inside the envelope are the following types of items:

- Parent handbook/Student handbook
- List of important names of people in the school
- Student government officer names and pictures
- Bell schedule/map of school
- Agenda planner (with handwritten welcome from principal would be a nice touch)
- Community pizza shop menu
- Principal and vice principal business cards
- School car magnet
- School store coupon
- Lunchroom snack coupon

It is a MUST that the principal meets and welcomes the student face to face. Making that connection is vital for the new student to connect with the school. Don't let the new student's first connection be with anyone else except the number-one supporter of the school, the principal. Additionally, the vice principal, guidance, head custodian, etc. can welcome the student.

Departing Students

When a student leaves the school, he/she wants others to notice that he/she left. Here are a few ways to let the student know that he/she will be remembered:

- Take his/her picture and post on a bulletin board. Title the board the "See You Soon" or "Still a Cougar" board.
- Have a page in the yearbook to highlight those who left during the year.
- Send a farewell text to the student.
- Make sure the student is signed up to get school notifications via email or text, so he/she knows what is going on.
- Get new address and send an invitation to student for homecoming.

5.6. Get Over It

Tall people get over being offended rather quickly because of the whole height thing. We get it all the time. People are always asking, "Do you play basketball? How's the weather up there? Could you get this off the top shelf? What's it look like up there?" Tall people get all of that talk so much that when people say it anymore, we really don't even worry about being offended. It's just not worth it. What are we going to do about it? Become small all of a sudden? Am I going to just shrink myself down to prevent it from happening? Respond when people say, "Oh, I wish I could have some of your height"? Seriously, let's think about this. I'm not going to give you any of my height. Even if I could. No! You wouldn't even know what to do with it. It's not worth the effort or the brain power to even address it.

That's the normal operation and thought process of tall people. When you transition this over to the world of leadership, you too really have to get over it. Stop worrying about being offended. Nobody can offend you. They can only give you the opportunity to be offended. Being offended is a choice. It's a choice that you make. You do not have to be offended when people say things to your or respond to you in a certain way that you feel that you're being disrespected. It's a choice whether this is going to affect you. What are you going to do with that opportunity of being offended or not?

Nobody can offend you. They can only give you the opportunity to be offended. #standtallstatement

It is important that when you are going through this process of whether you're going to be offended, you have an understanding of what offense really is and what offense can do to you as a Stand Tall Leader.

5.6.1. Offense Is a Constant Possibility

There's no way to truly know what every person is thinking, feeling, or has experienced. Therefore, the possibility of that offense to take place will always be there. When you're responding to someone or someone's responding to you, they don't know what the background is. They don't know what their experiences are. What is it that's digging at them? What is the thing that sets them off? Nobody knows it. So that offense possibility is always there. Now, in the past, we would rely a lot on common sense to guide our words and our directions as to how we interact with others so that we do not have that possibility of offense. But to be honest, nowadays, common sense isn't common anymore. It's hard to keep up with the approved norms of what's considered to be common. A lot of times you may say, ""If they had common sense, they wouldn't have said that. . .," or "If they had common sense, I wouldn't have been offended. . ." What you consider to be common isn't common anymore. What we consider common has spread so wide and far that for one person, it's one thing and another person, it's another. Therefore, offense is a constant possibility. If you understand and know that the possibility of offense is going to be always present, you can then make the decision whether you're going to step into that offense and allow it to bother you.

Common sense isn't common any more. #standtallstatement

5.6.2. Offense Is Attractive

Have you ever noticed that when someone states that they've been offended, everyone else tunes in? Someone states, "I was offended." Then instantly other chime in, "Oh really? What was it?" You want to know what the juicy gossip is. Offense is the starting point of some of the juiciest gossip out there. People love to take your offense and place it within their own moral standard to see how it measures up. Remember, everyone has their own set of experiences and life happenings, so therefore within their understanding of what exactly has happened may be different. They love to see the attractiveness of something, or someone being offended, and then put it into their own world. By putting it into their own moral compass in the world, they are going to ramp up that offense even higher. After that, you know what happens. They talk about the comparison of what your offense is to you as opposed to them. That is attractive. It's interesting. It's juicy, and it's entertaining. When you allow that opportunity of offense to come into your life and you have chosen to take on that offense, and especially if you share that offense with others, keep in mind, that is attractive. What other people do with the knowledge of the offense that you shared can turn out to be so much more of an issue and problem.

People love to take your offense and place it within their own moral standard to see how it measures up. #standtallstatement

5.6.3. Offense Ensnares Forward Movement

Tell me anything good that has come out of someone being offended. Mostly, offense puts a screeching halt to any progress or success. Rarely do you make the choice of becoming offended, embrace it, and then great things come out of it right away. It completely puts a halt to the thinking process, the progression process, and the growth process. It stops the time and energy it takes from the desired outcomes, and the necessary work is crippled. Even if there is a continued forward movement, eventually it is ensnared in offense and rarely moves smoothly. Even when it is over, the reflection of your offense that took place will always be there. It prevents forward movement at the pace it deserves to move.

> **Offense puts a screeching halt to any progress or success. #standtallstatement**

5.6.4. Offense Is Divisive

What do you really deserve? What do you really want? Are you on the path to getting what it is that you want? Offense can divide what it is you want and could ultimately give you only a part of it. This mostly happens when you are at the end of a project or event. You want to celebrate success of what you've accomplished and reflect on that process, but here comes offense creeping back in to divide the full enjoyable experience from happening. Allowing offense to take place prevents that fullness of understanding of what has just happened. It divides out what exactly the full outcomes and goals really need to be. Obtaining your desired outcomes is always something that you're striving for, but when you allow offense to creep in, it's going to chip away from what the desired outcome could be.

> **Offense can divide what it is you want and ultimately give you only a part of it. #standtallstatements**

Now that you have an understanding of what exactly offense is, the goal is to figure out how to get over offense. As much as I may say being offended is a choice, it is still a tough choice. We are talking about emotions here. We're talking about past experiences. We're talking about previous expectations that may have been broken. All of that and more are pulling into that offense. Ultimately, you have to make a decision. Even if the decision is that you will embrace that offense, you will eventually have to get over it in order to lead successfully. Therefore, here is how to get over that offense.

5.6.5. The Identity of the Past Does Not Determine the Identity of the Future

Whatever has happened in your past does not have to determine what is going to be in the future. Yes, you may have been offended in the past, and this new situation is similar to what has happened before. Amazingly, you are instantly pulled back to that previous event. But what has happened in the past doesn't have to determine how you're going to move forward.

> **What has happened in the past doesn't have to determine how you're going to move forward in the future. #standtallstatement**

In the 1600s when England would capture a pirate ship, it would christen that pirate ship and give it a new name. No matter what was done in the past by that ship, it would be forgiven and taken under the allegiance of the king and given a new name. Remember, don't let the past identify who you are and what it is that you do moving forward. If something comes into the forefront that may offend you, you do not have to roll back to those previous situations and events to allow that offense to gain strength.

5.6.6. The Risk of Remaining the Same Is Greater than the Perceived Risk of Changing

> **We always talk about how we need to change and evolve, but we tend to want that to happen to everyone else, not us.**
> **#standtallstatement**

Remaining the same and being a person that grabs offense and holds on to it for dear life is not a good thing. We always talk about how we need to change and evolve, but we tend to want that to happen to everyone else, not us – especially as it relates to being offended and holding onto offense. If you're going to remain the same and hold onto that risk of being someone who is offended all the time, then YOU are the one who needs to change. Think, I need to have a greater risk. Think, I need to have a greater opportunity to make this better. Think about how things have turned out in the past when you were offended and how things could change in the future by *not* holding onto that offense. That's the goal. You need to make the change within you. It has to be purposeful, and it has to be meaningful.

5.6.7. Be Aware of Your Position

As I have said, being tall means everyone sees you. You don't blend in. Everyone's watching what you do and what you don't do. Many times you may forget that as a leader. Then when you embrace offense, as much as you may try to hide it, others are going to see it on you. They are watching how you respond to that offense. Others will start to mimic those actions and the things that you do. If you are someone who goes off and yells and complains because you are offended, guess what happens when others under you get offended? They mimic those actions of that leader. It's like you are giving them permission to behave that way.

If you are someone who says, I'm not going to let that bother me and we're going to continue on in a positive way," then they're going to say, the leader didn't let the offense bother them and they're going to continue on. If you're someone who says, I'm going to address that at a later time. Let's keep this movement moving forward. Then they may do the same. We all know that it's not a guarantee that they're going to do exactly as you do, but the probability of them moving more in a direction that you are moving is higher. Keep in mind that what it is that you do ultimately affects all those around you. You want to develop an environment that continually moves in a positive direction. You are the one who establishes the behavioral culture that is either in alignment with what you say you respect and value or not in alignment with what you say you respect and value.

I'm sure you heard a thousand times over that it comes from the top. It comes from the leadership. It comes from how the leadership is behaving. It's all about how the leadership is acting. It's how the leadership is responding. Leaders will determine how those under them will react. That continual action frames the overall school. You are the center line of respect and values. Don't let negativity or offense be the norm of your school.

Don't let a negativity or offense be the norm of your school.
#standtallstatement

5.7. The Power of Now

Get to work, and you do what is necessary in the allotted time you have. If you wait too long, things are going to pass you by. But the argument comes into play as to maximizing and utilizing the time that you have. When consulting school leaders, one of the top things that they talk about is the inability to maximize the time they have and the ability to "get it all done." As much as you say you want to do things now, we all understand how the job works. "Now" comes and goes very quickly. You have to be aware and understand what time is really like and then what is the purpose of that time you have. Additionally, understand where your power comes from when you maximize the *power of now*. Therefore, what we are going to do to focus on a little bit of time and purpose, and your power of the time that you have? First, there's four things about time that you need to understand:

1. Time is not your enemy, but your ally.
2. Time is the great equalizer.
3. Time has limits.
4. Time has purpose.

5.7.1. Time Is Not Your Enemy, but Your Ally

Time only works against you when you underutilize it. It's not your enemy. I was a school administrator for several years and I struggled with this daily. I always found it amazing how time seems to fight against me when trying to complete the things that I need to do. I just don't have enough time to do all of these things on my list. This just isn't right. I'm always fighting against it. What I started to realize is that I needed to utilize my schedule and resources better – those who were assisting me, mainly my secretary and administrative team, and scheduling everything on my calendar. Having a list of things to do during the day just gives me additional stress. My list soars over my head like a flock of vultures ready to feed on my overstressed body. I am still fighting time to find when I will do each of the items on the list. I would find a moment when I could go to my office and start on my list and I would spend at least two to three minutes trying to decide what to tackle. I would usually pick the wrong thing to work on, because I really wouldn't have the amount of time to work on it. Sound familiar? Once I realized that scheduling the time specifically to do each item on the list within my calendar, I was able to remove the additional level of stress I had to find the time to do what was on the list. Between my secretary and I we were able to pinpoint my working style and understand how long it would take me to complete specific tasks. Additionally, we were able to schedule in wiggle room for those unexpected events and occurrences.

Time is not your enemy but your ally.
#standtallstatement

Think of how we expect teachers' lesson plans to be fluid and change according to the needs of the students. Your calendar can be created with enough open time to allow for fluidity when unexpected events occurred. Time only works against you when you underutilize it. You have to manipulate time the appropriate way so it is not your enemy but your ally. It will allow you to set limits on the number of things that you're going to do within an hour, half day, full day, week, and month. Using time in this way prevents you from spending too much time on one thing and not enough time on another. Embrace it and stop allowing time to be your enemy.

Stand Tall Action

Look at your to-do list. Look at your calendar. Move your to-do list to specific times within your calendar. Share your list with your secretary or someone who will support your time. Don't lie to yourself and not stick to it.

5.7.2. Time Is the Great Equalizer

Believe it or not, everyone has the same amount of time. It's about prioritizing that time. I remember looking at other administrators and I was just amazed at how they're able to do so much within their time. I'm looking at my three-ring circus and I don't think that I'm getting anything done! Nobody has any more time than anybody else. Everybody has the same amount of time. It's just how you prioritize that time and how you maximize your use of that time. Once I understood clearly that the other people around me have the same amount of time and they are just prioritizing their time according to what they believe is important, I started to really maximize my time and make sure that it was efficient.

Believe it or not, everyone has the same amount of time. #standtallstatement

5.7.3. Time Has Limits

It is not negotiable of how much time there is. There are only 24 hours in a day. There are 60 seconds in a minute. Time has a limit. It only goes so far. To be honest with you, everyone understands the rules of time. They just don't like the rules! Get over it! By understanding the rules of time, you can start to embrace the rules of time. You can begin to realize what you can do within that space. What is your working style? How can you use your calendar to strengthen your effectiveness within that time and space? It's important that on the front end you take the necessary time to think about how much time there really is for what you want to do. I get it – you don't have the time to even think about it to start with. Do it anyway. When you take that time to think of it at the start, it will ultimately make the rest of the time you use so much better.

There are only 24 hours in a day. There are 60 seconds in a minute. Time has a limit. It only goes so far. #standtallstatement

5.7.4. Time Has a Purpose

There is a reason to do things in the moment. You cannot understand your purpose until you understand the problem. Understand what the problems are will allow you to understand what your purpose is in the time that you have. That's when things start taking shape. What is understanding your purpose?

- Understand what your job is.
- Understand your role.

- Understand who is involved.
- Understand where the problem came from.
- Understand what the probable outcomes could be.
- Understand your WHY.
- Understand the expected outcomes.
- Understand what you respect and value.
- Understand the culture and climate.

The question is this: What is your purpose within your time now? Remember, time is not fighting against you. It can be your ally. It's the equalizer, and you have no more or less than anyone else around you. Understanding the limits of time can allow you to truly understand its purpose. Once you understand your purpose within that time, then you can solve those problems that come your way more efficiently and effectively (see below). So again, what is your purpose in your time now? The problem you are trying to solve is always bigger than the person you think you are. Once you get through the strongholds that are in your way, that's when you realize how big you really are.

Have you ever noticed when you finally get through a problem or you finally solve something that's happened? You can step back and think it through and realize, "Wow, I really did that!" It's okay to give yourself a pat on the back when you've gotten through tough problems. You have to think of those moments and those times that you've made those solving moments to reassure yourself, motivate yourself, inspire yourself to keep it going. Know that your purpose is always opportunity driven, not responsive. Think about your purpose and what it is that you are meant to do within your time of now.

A major guide to your purpose is what you respect and value. Remember, you are the center line of what the school respects and values. This should be the exact guide toward your purpose of time. When you are working within your time, always keep the importance of respect and value as the center of your actions. When taking your to-do-list and placing it within your calendar, the areas of respect and value should guide how you place the items within your calendar.

You are the commercial to your purpose and to your school. A commercial, as you know, is an advertisement to others about what your outcomes, processes and results. Being a Stand Tall Leader, you are always putting forward a commercial. You are showing other people why they are following you. You are living

You are the center line of what the school respects and values.
#standtallstatement

embodiment of the respect and values of the school. Why are you important? What is your commercial saying? Who is seeing your commercial? Showcasing your purpose in the time that you have showcases the best kind of commercial. You are the commercial to your purpose. Now is the time.

> Stand Tall Action
>
> Post what you respect and value within your office or workspace. Reflect on it when scheduling your time.

5.8. Efficiency vs. Effectiveness

What is the difference between efficiency and effectiveness, and why does it matter?

Efficiency is how quickly something gets done. When thinking of efficiency, you are concerned with the time frame allotted to complete the task. You want the task to be easy and with as little effort as possible. Efficiency is when we use tools and supports to get things done quickly. An example would be texting on your phone. It is a very efficient way to communicate with anyone at any time.

Efficiency = Doing Things Right

Effectiveness is how well something gets done. When thinking of effectiveness, you are concerned with the quality of the task. It does not matter how long it takes or how much effort it took, it just needs to be done well. Effectiveness is when we want the very best and we will forgo the use of tools at times to get an amazing outcome. An example would be building a piece of furniture from a kit. You must take your time, follow the instructions, and carefully put the pieces together according to the instructions, or it may not look or operate to its best ability.

Effectiveness = Doing the Right Things

Here's the thing about efficiency and effectiveness. We want both to happen all the time, and it is difficult to find that balance. Yes, we want to have the best outcomes and results, but we are limited with time. This is the basis of most complaints that teachers have within the classroom. They want to provide the very best teaching and learning opportunities, but they only have a limited amount of time to do it. Where is the middle ground where both efficiency and effectiveness are maximized? As a leader, this is where we struggle the most. We must push those who follow us to do things within a time frame that is sensible and to produce quality that may not fit within the allotted time frame that we give them.

In order to increase your probability of hitting the sweet spot with your decisions that is in the middle of efficiency and effectiveness, you need to understand what makes up each.

Formula for Efficiency

Efficiency = Expertise + Execution

In order to be fully efficient, you must have the necessary training, understanding, knowledge, and expertise within your area of interest. I'm sure you would agree that going into something with no knowledge will slow down your outcomes significantly and basically waste time. There are different levels of expertise, depending on the situation and person. Also, you must be able to execute that expertise well. You may know everything there is to know about great instructional practices, but unless you are able to execute and use them it means nothing. Both expertise and execution is necessary to be fully efficient. As a Stand Tall Leader, your job is to provide the necessary training to yourself and those who follow you that hit both increasing the expertise and strengthening the execution.

Formula for Effectiveness

Effectiveness = Efficiency + Emotion

In order to be fully effective, you must master efficiency first. Effectiveness will be nonexistent if there isn't the appropriate amount of knowledge through training and showcasing that training through execution. Think of your worst teachers who are completely ineffective. What is the first thing you do to help them? Provide training. Basically, attempt to increase their level of expertise and ability to showcase that expertise through execution. Once the person has the efficiency, they must want to do it well. There must be a desire to be the best. They have to understand what you respect and value and then use that knowledge to guide them in their actions moving forward. That is when you will find the optimum balance between effectiveness and efficiency.

Effectiveness is another example of the difference between *commitment* and *compliance*. Yes, someone can be effective through the act of being compliant. A teacher will teach the lesson with their knowledge and ability. Just imagine the level of effectiveness a teacher would have if they were committed to what was respected and valued within the school? Not only would they be in compliance, but they would be able to thrive and get results that were second to none.

> Efficiency = Doing Things Right
>
> Effectiveness = Doing the Right Things
>
> #standtallstatement

Stand Tall Action

Make a list of the daily management tasks that you have to do as a leader. First, go through that list and determine if your actions to complete that task is the most efficient way to do it. Second, go through that list and determine if your actions to complete that task are the most effective way to do it. In the end, see if you have any additional time or better outcomes.

Stand Tall Ideas

Dress-Down Monday

The title of this idea says it all. Typically, schools and companies offer dress-down Fridays. There is nothing wrong with that. It is a great way to celebrate a hard week of work and prepare for a fun weekend. On dress-down Friday, people are feeling good as if nothing can bother them for the day. The weekend is looking good and all is well.

Just think of what would happen if on Friday afternoon an email or an announcement was made by the principal that Monday is a dress-down day. Instantly, people would start popping out of their rooms like gophers from the ground, buzzing with each other about the dress-down day for Monday. All of the sudden, people are dancing in the hallways, skipping to their cars, and going out for drinks. The weekend is full of vigor and anticipation for the upcoming workweek. The best thing is that everyone is ready for Monday to come.

Usually, Monday is a day that drags, and people are not full of much energy. But on dress-down Monday, people are upbeat and comfortable. What a great way to start off the week! Keep in mind that you don't want to pull this card out that often. When you see that things are tense or stress levels are getting high is a good time to use a dress-down Monday. Talk to your school or company leadership and try it out. It doesn't cost a thing! Let me know how it goes.

Birthday Ambush

My students came up with this idea in order to celebrate the teachers' birthdays. I gave the student leader of the group a list with the name of each teacher and his or her birthday (not including the year). A small group of students get together in the morning and ambush the teacher in his or her classroom with a happy birthday song. Following the song, they would slap a poster on the door that says, "I've been birthday ambushed! Happy Birthday!"

After the first three teachers got ambushed, it caught on like wildfire. Teachers were excited and could not wait for their turn. Even the teachers who have birthdays during the summer were checking in to see when they would get their ambush. It was a simple little thing, but it went a long way because the kids recognized their birthdays and left a poster so they would get good wishes all day.

Support the Support

Support staff is vitally important to the success of the school. Custodians, food service, classroom aides, bus drivers have extremely important jobs. If any of them were unable to do their job, the entire place would fall apart. Additionally, they can provide great information to the community about your school. Therefore, they should always be kept in the loop. They should know what is going on and what their role is in the bigger picture.

Give Them the Stuff

Make sure they get the parent newsletter, staff newsletter, all email messages, staff handbook, phone messages, and text alerts. They should receive it the same day as everyone else. They should never be considered an afterthought.

Meetings

If you are able to, invite them to the regular faculty meeting. If you are unable to, schedule a special meeting for them. I schedule a standing support staff meeting every month. It is completely voluntary. Some months I have a full house, some months I have two people. Either way, I am there with an agenda and quality information.

Come See Me

The principal should schedule a time every month when support staff can visit with the support staff. It is a clearly advertised time that is just for support staff to communicate with the principal about whatever they wish.

Training

If possible, provide professional development on public relations for support staff. Often, support staff is the first encounter with the community. Make sure it is a good one.

Within Disney World, the street cleaners are trained on customer service more than any other position. The reason is because they are mixed within the public more than any other position. Therefore, they are approached by more people and are asked more questions than anyone else. Disney realized that they want to make every experience within the parks magical, even talking with support staff.

Good Citizen of the Month 2.0

This is a twist on something that a lot of schools do. Often schools have criteria for citizen of the month and they only share it with the staff so they can secretly look for students who fit that criteria. When the student is announced, it is a big surprise. Here is the switch: Post the criteria for citizen of the month everywhere! Talk to the students about how important this honor is, and what is needed to become a student of the month. The teachers should talk about it often and highlight those who are emulating the aspects of good citizenship. The end result is that more students start to show the behaviors of good citizenship in the hope of winning the honor. True, there are those who will not care at all, but there are also those who will start moving in that direction, trying to get the award. Another option is to have former citizens of the month talk to the incoming freshmen or students about the importance of the award and what they did/do to get and keep the honor.

CHAPTER · SIX
Stand Tall Leaders Take Action

6.1. BADASS

This section is about taking the next steps of being a Stand Tall Leader and truly going above and beyond. Many books revolve around the BADASS brand. Jen Sincero has written several BADASS books. This is my version of being a BADASS as it relates specifically to be a Stand Tall Educational Leader. BADASS is an acronym for being:

Bold
Action Focused
Decisive
Aware
Smart
Systematic

6.1.1. Bold

Do you know what you stand for? What is it that you will not waiver from? Being strong, confident, and secure in your own vision, knowledge, and actions is hugely important as it relates to being a Stand Tall Educational Leader. You want those you lead to know you as someone who doesn't move from what your beliefs are.

Earlier, we discussed about the importance of integrity. Integrity is a set of beliefs, values, and actions that others can depend on. If you have strong beliefs, values, and actions that others can depend on and you don't move from it, others will know that those are the cornerstones of your leadership. That determines and defines the boldness you demonstrate as a leader. You know what you stand for. You let others know what you stand for, respect, and value. Here is the kicker – then you live it!

We talked about the results formula earlier. The first part of making sure that you get the results is identifying what it is that you respect in your school and identifying what you respect in the classroom. Being a BADASS leader means that you are identifying and clearly know what you respect for yourself. To get the results that you want for yourself, you must understand what it is and be bold enough to let others know. Make it clear as day what it is you respect personally, and Stand Tall.

> **Being a BADASS leader means that you are identifying and clearly know what you respect for yourself.**
> **#standtallstatement**

When you go through your day, walking in the hallways and interacting with others, your Integrity should ooze out of you from every poor. Others should be able to see and feel it even when walking past you in the hallways. Tall people who embrace being tall stand erect – shoulders square, chest out, head up. They walk with a little bit of a swagger. They walk with confidence. There's a difference between confidence and arrogance. Arrogance is confidence out of control, while confidence is arrogance under control. You want to be on the fine line between the high end of confidence and the lower end of arrogance. Others should see you as a leader. Be bold, be strong, be confident as to what it is that you are about. Make sure you speak up for what you believe in. Let everyone know this is what you're about at all times.

Arrogance is confidence out of control, while confidence is arrogance under control. #standtallstatement

6.1.2. Action Focused

Do what you say you are going to do. This is also a part of the process of maintaining your Integrity. If you're going to be a BADASS leader, you have to put your Integrity into action. We talked earlier about the four ways to be action focused. It is important that you step into that and you do what you say you're going to do. If you make plans, you must go through the process to get it done. Set realistic timelines for when you can get things done. Set timelines that are a little longer and then get the work done sooner. That's how others will start to say, that this leader knows her stuff, she gets it done, and she does it through her actions. You can give as much lip service as possible, but if you're not stepping into the actions and making it happen, what good are you?

Hold yourself accountable more than others are holding you accountable. Be the one that motivates and inspires yourself to do what is necessary. Try to think of yourself in the third person. If you need to, get in front of the mirror and talk to yourself. Do it! Take the actions and then let others know what your process is. Many times, as leaders the actions that we do in schools, we try to do in secret. We do them in secret for a couple of reasons. One, we do it so that we do not get feedback or criticisms from others. We believe they want to judge what it is that we do. Two, if we don't let others know how we are doing in our progress, it gives us some wiggle room to not necessarily move forward at the pace others are holding us to and therefore, you don't have to deal with that judgment. If you are a BADASS leader in a school, letting others know your progress is the norm. You are holding yourself accountable and they are also holding you accountable. The level of respect you gain from others increases dramatically. You don't want to not do what's necessary. You don't want to let them down. As a BADASS Leader you are showing others that you are not just in compliance but you are committed. So be a BADASS. Let them know your progress. It reassures others and keeps the movement forward.

You can give as much lip service as possible, but if you're not stepping into the actions and making it happen, what good are you? #standtallstatement

6.1.3. Decisive

> **For the love of the almighty, make a decision and stick with it!**
> **#standtallstatement**

For the love of the almighty, make a decision and stick with it! The most upsetting complaint to have from staff about a leader is when a leader can't make a decision. So, when you are making a decision, be confident of that decision. Don't be vague. Be specific. Say, this is the decision, and when necessary, say this is why you made that decision. Earlier, we referenced the five levels of decision making. There are times when making a decision is all on you. There are other times when decisions are going to involve other people. If you are utilizing the levels of decision making, you must stick to the process and the decision. It strengthens your integrity. It strengthened your commitment. It strengthened your BADASS-ness so that you are that high-level Stand Tall Leader that others can look up to.

Yes, you may make a decision that others don't like. But they respect the fact that you made the decision and stuck with it. There should not be a question as to what you mean. Again, don't be vague. Be specific. It is almost as frustrating to have a leader give a vague description of the decision being made. Equally, if there are multiple possible outcomes, allow room for revisiting the decision for a more definitive answer, and provide a timeline for when that would happen. People respect that. Let others know your timeline. Build that level of trust. You work with professionals. Teachers have a college degree; they are dedicated to the children. So allowing your staff to be aware of the timelines, letting them be aware of the obstacles, saying what we are doing, saying why we are doing it, and saying how we are doing it helps keep you accountable as a BADASS leader. It helps your team have a sense of security. It builds trust. So be decisive, get to the point, know what your decision is going to be. Just make a decision and stick with it.

> **Yes, you may make a decision that they don't like. But they can respect the fact that you made the decision and stuck with it.**
> **#standtallstatement**

6.1.4. Aware

One thing that I was guilty of is not paying attention to things that I was not interested in as a leader. A lot of different things happen in schools and in districts, and to be perfectly honest with you, it's difficult to stay on top of it all. But as a leader you really, truly need to be aware of things that are happening that you are not interested in. You may make excuses by thinking, I'm okay if I don't know it.

Unfortunately, when certain issues and concerns would come up, I would have to relearn everything because I was not aware from the start. I felt that I was unable to make realistic, sensible, informed decisions. Basically, I would fake it till I made it, because I truly didn't understand what was going on. I had to rely on others and what they were doing in order to make it. Sometimes those who I would rely on would not step up.

If you are a BADASS leader in a school, you are more aware of what is going on. Be attentive to all that is happening in your school or district. Be purposeful about being updated on what is happening. Whether it's weekly meetings with specific groups or one-on-one consultations, use your assistants to make sure that you are aware and updated so you can react and respond appropriately when needed.

You are a conduit. By being aware and connected, you can make sure that all the different areas within your school or district are properly connected to what you respect and value. Remember, the results formula is about focusing everything around what it is that you respect and value. If you remain aware of what's going on, you can make sure that everything is in alignment. This is how you maintain and strengthen your culture so that your climate remains more consistent around your values. If you want to get the results that you want, you need to make sure that things are in alignment. Make sure they connect to what the organization is about. Stepping back and not being aware can ultimately become problematic and detrimental. Be aware.

Be purposeful about being updated on what is happening. #standtallstatement

6.1.5. Smart

Be smart! This means making sure that as a Stand Tall BADASS Leader you are continually growing. Being a leader is busy. It is very, very busy! There are so many things that you have to do on a given week, day, hour, or minute. I am sure, like me, there are days you look at the list of things to do and wonder how in the world you can get it all done. On top of that, you need to be the instructional leader of your building. As you know, there are so many things that get in the way of you continually stepping into that role. You must be purposeful in making sure that you increase your professional development and the knowledge that you have so that you remain Smart.

When thinking of professional development as a school leader, think of professional development differently. You don't have to have professional development solely by reading a book, taking a course, or attending a conference. Those are all great ways to increase your knowledge and to become super smart within your area of leadership, but another option is to find multiple avenues to network with other administrators.

Networking should be about connecting with others to help improve yourself and improve other people. Joining social media groups is a great way for that to happen. Attend an online summit, where multiple speakers or trainers provide insights. You might be able to participate in a live conference in this way or watch a prerecorded event. There are more and more podcasts and trainings available for administrators and school leaders that truly focuses on the needs and specifics of the school leaders. Also, there are leadership and training courses outside of the area of education that are extremely valuable. Think about how they can help you become better in what it is that you do.

Consider an online mastermind group or developing a mastermind group within your own area. Mastermind groups are great because they allow multiple people with multiple but related backgrounds to get together and you can brainstorm and share ideas. An online mastermind group is the best way to go. I've developed a Stand Tall Mastermind where school leaders from all around the country take one hour a week and log in online through video conferencing. They get a quick mini-lesson on leadership and then they share what it is that they're doing to get results and solutions. Within a Mastermind, a principal in Oklahoma might be helping an educator in North Carolina. A school leader in Alabama might have a solution for something that might be happening in Michigan. The great part is that now they are all connecting together. To me, that is true professional development. That is being Smart! So now when you walk into your school, you are providing solutions, insights, and new ideas. You are smart. You are that BADASS leader.

You must be purposeful in making sure that you increase your professional development and the knowledge that you have so that you remain smart. #standtallstatement

6.1.6. Systematic

Develop patterns and systems of how things will work. When you are developing new ideas, solutions, and programs, be very systematic about how it's going to roll out and take place. Also, make sure it is in alignment to what you respect and value. Being systematic directly connects with your scheduled culture.

The number-one statement we hear when we are implementing new programs, making some adjustments, or making changes is, "How are you going to get buy in?" "How are we going to get the teachers to get involved?" From that, we usually come up with a couple little scoopy ideas and throw them to the wall to see what sticks. Come on! You know that's not going to work all the time. That isn't a strategy. The goal is to increase the probability of success. When a company puts out a new product, what do they do? They get together and develop a marketing team on how it's going to be introduced. How it's going to be presented? What is it going to look like? How often are they going to show this to the people? What is the feedback we are expecting to get? When you are rolling something out and you are trying to put things into place, you must be systematic and purposeful in order to be the successful Stand Tall BADASS Leader.

How is this new process, adjustment, or change going to roll out? How often are we going to talk about it? What else are we're going to do? When change takes place, sometimes it takes up to seven points of contact before people are comfortable with that change. Because of that timeline, it is going to take a while to think it through. By being systematic in your process, over time you increase the probability of others moving from complying with the adjustment or change to being committed to the adjustment or change.

Quality systems develop quality culture. Systems are something that is not developed to be implemented one time. A system is developed to be used over time. Culture is a fancy word for traditions, and traditions happen over time. So be systematic, schedule your systems, stick to your systems and be a BADASS leader in your school.

Quality systems develop quality culture.
#standtallstatement

Stand Tall Action

What are you doing to be a BADASS Stand Tall Leader? Each month, pick one of the letters in the acronym and add an action you will do to make that a reality in your life. Once at the end, start again. This will give you a goal for each month for one year. At the end of the year, look back and see how much better of a BADASS Stand Tall Leader you are!

Stand Tall Ideas

Headers and Footers

Educators are the kings and queens of paper. We send home papers for a wide variety of reasons – everything from announcement of the field trip to a study guide before the big test. Many are now moving toward using electronic documents in order to "save a tree" or two. Either way, most

(*Continued*)

documents have a header and a footer. A header is the space at the top of the document and the footer is the space at the bottom. These two spaces are golden for the educator. Within this space you can put a wide variety of information that you want to relay to your students or family. For starters, within the footer of *every* document you send home to parents should have the following:

- Full name
- Contact Information
- Best time to contact you or prep times

By providing this information on every document that goes home, you are training your students and parents on how and when to contact you. It will quickly streamline your communication with your parents.

Additional information to place in the header or footer of documents:

- Quote of the week
- Important dates
- Clue to a question
- Classroom website address
- QR code
- School website address
- How to sign up for classroom text
- Extra credit
- Headshot photo
- Mascot image

The goal is to ensure important information is always available all the time on every document that goes home. Your students and parents will start being trained to look to the header or footer for important information. When the time comes that they need to contact you or the school, they can pull out any document from any point throughout the school year and know what to do.

Positive Office Referral

When a student misbehaves, he/she is written up on an office referral form, which has been designed to provide clarification to the office of what the infraction was. There are categories that determine how serious of an action it was and guidance on how to handle it. Usually only students getting in trouble are called to the office. With a positive office referral, staff can write up any student for doing the right thing. The positive office referral form categorizes good behavior so the office can understand what was done. I asked the teachers to send at least one positive office referral a month, but most did two or three. The office administrator would call down students (one at a time) and ask them if they knew why they were there. Most of the time, they had no idea and were on the verge of crying. The administrator would read the positive referral and praise the student for his or her actions. It is important to call the student's parent while the student is in the office, then share the news with the parent and pass the phone to the student so they can talk. On many occasions, everyone in the room and on the phone was in tears. During the recognition rally, all the students who received positive office referrals were recognized again.

Locker Mission Messages

One school year, the theme for my building was *Anything's Possible*. With that theme we focused our design around secret agents and the *Mission Impossible* movies. To start the school year on a positive note, we put a "mission" in every student's locker. Every student got a special "mission" message the first time they opened their locker.

Each of the mission statements were on small, colorful paper. They had the theme design and a simple message to encourage them. We came up with 20 different missions. Our goal was to provide a variety of messages so students would not have the same one as the neighbor next to them. Some of the messages:

- Stay focused on your work.
- Say hello to someone new.
- Thank your teacher every day.
- Read a genre that you usually would not read.
- Take a chance.
- Thank the cafeteria workers.

Before the students were assigned the locker, they were told about the theme for the year and that a "mission" will be provided to them in the lockers. Throughout the first two weeks of school, students were randomly asked if they completed their mission. Surprisingly, many of them said yes. This idea is a great way to focus the students around your theme for the year.

6.2. One Action

Take action! It's important as a Stand Tall Leader you step up and take action for what it is that you need to do. As we have said before, one of the things that bothers teachers and people who follow leaders more than anything is when leaders don't step up and take action to make things happen. You need to get results. One action can not only save a life but can also change the world. As a leader there are many actions that you do that make a huge impact on others. Do all actions with Integrity. When a former student or former parent comes to you and shares something you did or how you behaved or how you acted that made an impact on their lives or their child's life. There is no better feeling in the world.

It's the actions that you do that mean the world to others. In my county, every year there is an annual countywide teacher appreciation luncheon for the teachers of the year for each of the individual schools and districts, held at the local military base and sponsored by the military. How great to truly recognize and see all the great teachers of the year throughout the county! The one time that I attended the event, I took my teacher of the year. We had a wonderful time. At the end, on the way out of the event, one of the teachers of the year from another school came over to me and said, "Oh my goodness, it's you. Are you Mr. Bollar?" I responded, "Yes, I am." She told me that her daughter had me as an art teacher when she was in third grade. I responded by asking her name. Blah, blah, blah. I did not remember what the girl's name was, or who she was. She continued to tell me that her daughter said that I made a significant impact in her life. How did I do that? She stated that her daughter had just been accepted into college, and her major is going to be art education. She chose art education because I was her art teacher and it made such an impact on her life. Her daughter made a determination way back in third grade that she was going to be an art teacher. I was floored! I gave her my card so her daughter could contact me. This is amazing. I just couldn't believe that this took place because of the actions I took and the decisions I made way back during my first few years of teaching.

I was able to step into those decisions and took action so that an impact was made on other's lives. That wasn't my goal, but that's what happened. Just one smile, one action, one act of helping, one word, one statement can change a person's life. It could make all the difference in the world. You can't change your past, but you can change your future. You can't change someone else's past, but you may be able to change their future. Take action, do what you say you're going to do.

I love the Disney movie *Chicken Little*. I love it because he takes action. He sets his mind to something and he goes for it. True, there are some mishaps and some crazy things happen along the way, but overall, he makes a huge impact. In one scene in the movie they play the song "One Little Step." It chronicles Chicken Little and how he is going to make it to school. It's all about taking action, being different, thinking and working through what needs to be done and stepping out and not being afraid to make it happen.

Your actions can influence the future.
#standtallstatement

6.2.1. One Action Can Release Your Potential

The actions that you take are like seeds. When you start the action, it's planting the progression of what's to come. Once that action is taken, you nourish it. You follow up with on it. You continue with it so that it can grow into something amazing. The potential of growth remains dormant until action is taken to place upon it. So, once you start something, you have that potential for growth. You have to go for it. When you have a thought, when you have a brainstorming session, when you sit in another meeting, when you come up with ideas – that's all potential for growth. You have to act on it in order for it to turn into something. You will never know how great or small the potential is until you act on it. Your negativity can release harm into other people, so you need to make sure that your actions are positive. The outcomes that you want to receive can take place. I have found that most ideas that people have in meetings, brainstorming sessions, and think tanks can work. The success revolves around the activity necessary to make it work. You can do this! It can happen! The question is, will you be a Stand Tall Leader and take the actions to make it happen?

The potential of growth remains dormant until action is taken to place upon it. #standtallstatement

6.2.2. Inactivity Is Passive Agreement

For example, don't just *talk about* random acts of kindness. Perform random acts of kindness. There are so many times in schools we come up with programs. We may call them concepts, things to improve the climate and culture, social emotional wellness. We push these programs onto the students as what the expectations are. The problem is that we don't take the actions necessary to make them reality. If you want to have a program where you are doing random acts of kindness and you are recognizing students for doing it well, then guess who else needs to do random acts of kindness? The leaders, teachers, and everyone in the school community. The point is to be the example. Why just do *random* acts of kindness? How about doing *intentional* acts of kindness? Say that you will do intentional acts of kindness, and then do it. It sets the standard. It allows for growth. It makes things stronger. You will never get the results that you want unless you are purposeful with your actions. Doing nothing and hoping that things get better isn't a strategy. Remember, Standing Tall means you don't blend in with others. They see who you are, what it is you are doing and what you are not doing. Be the example through your actions. Release your potential and the potential of your school through your actions.

You will never get the results that you want unless you are purposeful with your actions. #standtallstatement

6.2.3. One Action Can Elicit Uncommon Responses

Have you ever seen somebody yawn? You see them open their mouth, lean back, maybe make a sound, stretch a little bit. Yaaaawwwnnn! As soon as you see a good yawn, you want to yawn. Some of you may have done it right now. It's contagious. It's something that moves through others. When you have an action, sometimes the outcome could be a contagious uncommon response. Different types of things happen because of that action. Things start to move. Have you ever witnessed the mob mentality when large group behavior spreads? The action of one person spreads and others get wrapped up into that behavior.

I have heard that it takes sometimes seven touches or connections with others for people to start feeling comfortable with connecting in order to start the sales process. This is done through email, phone, face to face. It's all about relationship building when dealing with sales. I believe it's the same thing as it relates to implementing new ideas or trying to allow for change to take place within your district or school. A lot of times we say that we want things to happen and we do some small action. Like providing a two-hour training. We want the outcomes to be there immediately. Those outcomes don't happen, and then we get frustrated because the people aren't getting the results. Sometimes you need to have multiple points of action and multiple points of connectivity with others so that those programs can take place. Here's an example. Let's say you want a new program that deals with instruction in some way, so let's look at the seven points of connection:

1. You talk about it at the faculty meeting, you introduce it, you explain it.
2. You share a link with the teachers so they can go in and they can connect with it in some way.
3. You have a webinar with the sales agent or with the instructional agent so that the teachers can log and get a little bit more information about it.
4. You have the trainer come in and do the professional development for the teachers.
5. You pilot the program. Some within your classrooms. Just one unit or a couple of lessons, so teachers can get a feel for it.
6. You have a discussion at the individual team meetings about what the program involves or what happened with the pilot.
7. You have a follow-up discussion with the team and the trainer.

Maybe at this point you may have people starting to become comfortable with the new instructional program that you're bringing in. Multiple actions can elicit uncommon responses.

You may be ready for change, but others aren't. You need to have many different actions in order to make sure that change happens. At times, the response may not be what you want without doing the work. The reinforcement within the results formula is a perfect example of how multiple touches are needed to get the results you want. *Reinforcement* is all about doing something again, and again, and again in order to strengthen what you *respect* and *value.*

Sometimes you need to have multiple points of action to get the results you want. #standtallstatement

6.2.4. One Action Can Reveal a Path to Wholeness

Have you ever had a new student teacher who was paired with a poor mentor teacher? I feel so sad for those teachers. Unknowingly the student teacher starts to model what it is that poor mentor teacher shared with them. Juxtaposed, you have a new student teacher that was paired with a phenomenal mentor teacher. It's amazing the difference. That student teacher mimics the actions of that excellent example. Even if that new student teacher was great on their own but was paired with a poor mentor teacher, there will be something lacking, and it's very obvious. Many people don't step up and simply model what they have seen or experienced. They take that action as truth. One action can break that curse. If someone has a continual pattern of behavior and actions that goes against what you respect, you need to take action. You need to say something. Step up and do something about it.

When you have staff who are just doing enough, that isn't enough. Remember, good is the enemy of great! Take the action to reveal the path to wholeness. What can you do to make the change for the better? Take the steps necessary to move them from noncompliance to compliance and from compliance to commitment. Stand in the gap and right the wrong that others are doing. That's what Stand Tall Leadership is all about: Making things right. Getting results. Aligning the actions within the school with what you respect and value. Rosa Parks. We all know the story. She stood in the gap of what was wrong so that the right thing could take place.

Is it going to be easy? No, but that's what your job is. One action can reveal the path to others. One action can reveal wholeness of the right way of correcting the wrongs. One action can move others toward the center line of what you respect and value. Students deserve amazing teachers and administrators who will model excellence for them.

Take the action to reveal the path to wholeness. #standtallstatement

6.2.5. One Action Can Restore or Rob the Future

Either you are a part of the problem or you're part of the solution. Your actions can make all the difference for the future. You can restore what was wrong or you can rob what's going to happen. Choose to be the Stand Tall Leader who serves by serving. Maintain a view of solutions. Focus on positive outcomes. Are you more concerned with being the man or woman who's in charge or the one who Influences others to be better? Make sure your focus is on solutions, positive outcomes, and what you respect and value most. If you are serving those that are under you, you want them to experience success. Yes, you may have to make some difficult decisions at times, but a servant mindset can restore a positive future for those you serve. The probability of the future being positive is so much higher because of your service.

It's difficult as a tall person to not have a little bit of an ego. I know there are many tall people who are very humble and such, but overall, tall people feel pretty good about being tall. You can see things others can't. You have advantages over others. There are some things that are not so great about being tall, but overall, it's not a bad gig. As a leader you should embrace the position you are in. Be proud of yourself. Stroke the ego a little. Keep in mind that as that leader you can restore and make sure that others are getting what they need; your position and actions can help their future. If you are not having the positive service mindset, you could be robbing another person's future of what it is that they can do.

Either you are a part of the problem or you're a part of the solution. Your actions cn make all the difference for the future. #standtallstatement

Stand Tall Ideas

Start of the School Year Ideas

- Have each homeroom decorate a flag to hang outside of the classroom to show unity.
- Have each classroom come up with a slogan or theme that focuses everywhere around a common goal.
- Bring the freshman into the school from a separate entrance and have upperclassmen cheer them through the hallways. Have some available to help them get to where they need to go following the cheering!
- Gather students outside and parade around the block of the neighborhood, celebrating the start of school.

- Have or create some "I survived the first week or day of school" stickers to give to the students at the end of the first day or week.
- Shows a finish-strong video to the seniors on the first day and give out buttons, T-shirts, or other wearable items that have the finish-strong logo as a theme for the remainder of the school year.
- Create a #hashtag specifically for the seniors; have the students post how they are going to make their senior year memorable. Take the responses and post them throughout the school or on the TV station in the school.
- Invite the local sports team mascot to be at the school to welcome students on the first day.
- Play fun, upbeat music throughout the school on the first day.
- Post positive goals throughout the school so students can use them as a guide to develop their own goals for the school year.
- Get a red-carpet runner at the front of the school to make it seem more important when the kids arrive on the first day.
- Have a limo place at the front of the school and allow students to walk through the limo and out the other side. It appears as if you are coming out onto the red carpet for the first day of school.
- Provide open-door valet service to the students for being dropped off by their parents in the car line. Simply have some people there to open the door for the students and welcome them to the school.
- Have volunteers hold up encouraging signs along the route to school for the first day of school. Signs might include "Welcome!" "Good luck!" positive quotes, or your theme for the school year.

School Theme Ideas

Personally, I love using a school theme each year. The purpose of the theme is to focus everyone around a common vision and goal. Additionally, it is fun to wrap events and activities around the theme throughout the year. The problem that many schools have with using a theme is they do not take the time prior to the school year to brainstorm and plan actions, events, and internal branding around the theme. The theme sounds great during the summer and the start of the year, but by November, nobody remembers it and it is barely discussed. Make sure that you systematically push

(*Continued*)

that theme throughout the school year. Give your staff talking points at least once a month to discuss with the students as it relates to the school. Come on! You can come up with 10 talking points. It's just one a month for 10 months. Use the theme on letterhead and at the start and end of announcements. Have it said at the start and finish of sporting and arts events. Seriously, what good is a theme if everyone forgets the theme? Little actions and planning can make the biggest impact.

50 + 1 School Theme Ideas

1. Wonder
2. Be Kind
3. Kindness Matters
4. Read, Lead, Succeed
5. Knowledge Is Power
6. Fit and Focused
7. Everything Is Awesome!
8. Education Is an Adventure (Camping)
9. Wizard of Oz. . . There's No Place Like (name of school)
10. Beetles "Come Together"
11. Dreamers
12. Kindness Rocks
13. Back 2 the Future
14. Be the One, or Be the Change
15. Cactus: Be Sharp and Stick Together
16. One Team, One School
17. Strong Alone, Unstoppable Together
18. Together We Ride
19. Charting the Course (compass/boat)
20. Full STEAM Ahead
21. Soaring to New Heights
22. Mission IS possible
23. Mission Possible

24. Success Under Construction
25. The Greatest School on Earth
26. Adventure Awaits
27. All Means All
28. Success Begins with Me
29. You Are the Missing Piece
30. Make It Count
31. Rock Your Role
32. Find Joy in the Journey
33. Be Legendary
34. Pride Is in Us All
35. Cool 2 Care
36. It's Up 2 U
37. Power Up to Success (Super Mario)
38. Let's Move Mountains
39. Wild, Wild Best
40. Adventure in Learning (Pirates)
41. This Is Me
42. Get in the Game
43. Build Excellence
44. REEL Them IN! (Relate Engage Empower Leverage)
45. Hustle and Heart Set Us Apart
46. Kindness Changes Everything
47. 1% Better Every Day
48. The Leader in Me
49. CAMP (Care About Making Progress)
50. HUGS (Helping Us Grow Schoolwide)
51. Good to Great to AWESOME

(*Continued*)

BYOB

BYOB stands for Bring Your Own Banana. This is a fun twist to a faculty meeting. Prior to the meeting, put a banana in each faculty member's mailbox. You can even write instructions on the banana that they must bring the banana with them to the faculty meeting. Once the teachers arrive at the faculty meeting, have ice cream and toppings available for them. Starting off the faculty meeting with everyone having a banana split is a great way to end the school day and start the meeting.

CHAPTER · SEVEN

Stand Tall Leaders Use Their Voice

7.1. Stand Tall Speaking

As a leader, it is important that you have top-notch communication skills. There are a lot of ways to communicate. There's communicating one-on-one, large groups, electronic communication, written communication, and social media communication. There are so many different ways to get your message across. One of the most-important areas to master is how well you speak publicly and address groups, audiences, or crowds. It's important that you are polished, succinct, and can truly connect with those around you.

I speak and train publicly over 100 times a year, and I am a chapter president of the Philadelphia Chapter of the National Speakers Association. Public speaking is a deep love of mine. I always find it interesting and also very sad when school leaders are not polished and able to speak well in public. Things can either happen or not happen based on the way the leader presents to others. If you are someone who can speak well – meaning, in a way that is thought provoking, gets to the point, and makes sure that others understand what's being said – there's so much more progress you can make as a leader.

> The first 30 seconds and the last 30 seconds of whatever you are saying have the most impact. You need to be aware of how you are starting and how you are going to end. Whether you are addressing the entire district, presenting to the board of education, or addressing the community, you have to start in a way that grabs their attention, provides impact, and gets them to want to listen. Then, when you close share words that are strong and meaningful.

Here are the top six things that you can do to improve your speaking and presentation skills as a Stand Tall Leader.

7.1.1. Get to the Point!

Always say something of interest before getting to business, but you want to make sure that the point is made. When you get to the point you need to make sure that it connects directly to what your outcomes need to be and has something that strengthens that point. It's a little buffer or precursor to the point. It allows people to digest what's going to be said, but don't take forever. Get to the point.

What is the audience thinking, based on who you are? Do they have an understanding of your position and what you do? How do they see you? Once they know this, it can help you when you're developing the proper words to use to get to the point.

Make sure you script your opening statement. Don't leave it to chance. Think of exactly what you are going to say. Be specific. Brevity is your friend. It takes time to come up with how you are going to state your intro or what your opening statement will be. Keep in mind again, your first 30 seconds and the last 30 seconds have the most impact. Own those first 30 seconds and *get to the point!*

Think about how you are branding yourself as a leader. What is it that you want others to understand? Use your intro as a way to make sure you are strengthening that brand. Different ways that you can do this:

- Start off with a quote and say it slowly so everyone can grasp the meaning. Memorize the quote and look at the audience when saying it. That way it is more impactful.
- State what you respect from the results formula. This can help reinforce what is most important in the school.
- Say a statement of assurance or affirmation. Again, memorize the statement and look directly at the audience when saying it.
- If your district or school has a certain branding statement, use that every single time you start your talk. Encourage the audience to join you quoting that statement.
- Use a poem that connects to the point or the culture of the school/district. I have a friend who is a professional speaker. He uses a poem every single time that he starts a speech. Over the years, others now know that poem and connect its meaning to him as a person.

If you are consistent with your openings, others start to realize that is who you are and what you are about. You are strengthening your level of Integrity by *speaking out for what you believe in*. It provides a sense of comfort. You are developing your brand. Just remember to not spend a ton of time on that opener and GET TO THE POINT!

Brevity is your friend. Get to the point!
#standtallstatement

7.1.2. Minimize the Verbal Junk

The written word is for the eye. The spoken word is for the rhythm. When creating your speech, keep in mind that how you write a speech is different than how you say a speech. A lot of times you write extra stuff knowing that it is pleasing to the eye and how it is read and transferred in the mind. But when you're speaking, you don't need as many words. Think about how it sounds. How does it flow? What words are interesting words to the ear? What words might be too much? Think about how you are saying what needs to be said and then edit. Edit not for the writing but edit for the listening of the words. Think of the patterns, speed, and targets of how you are saying things. Do you need to slow down at certain points and be very specific? Do you need to speed up through lists so that it sounds good when you are saying it? If it's a joke, practice saying the joke (*especially if you are not funny*). Think about pausing for longer periods of time because people many need to process what was said. However you are going to do it, make sure you look at it based on how it sounds not written and then get rid of all the extra verbal junk that is not necessary.

People will appreciate you getting to the point, clearing out all the extra fluff. Do the best you can to get rid of those little sounds we all make when we talk: Ummm, Uhhh, You See, Hmmm, Ahhh, Shhhh. We say those things when we are talking casually, but when you are addressing others, get rid of the verbal junk and you will sound amazing.

The written word is for the eye. The spoken word is for the rhythm.
#standtallstatement

7.1.3. Use Stories

Stories connect with people. Stories are the currency of human contact. These are the things that make whatever it is that needs to be said meaningful. Finding stories is not hard to do. There are tons of ways that you can grab stories to strengthen your point. You can reference a story from history. There are thousands of stories throughout history that can strengthen the points that need to be made. There are millions of stories that take place in schools. Maybe you have a story from your personal life. Providing stories of your personal life strengthens your brand. It strengthens your relationship with others around you. Your audience will think they know you better. Through your stories it makes leadership work so much easier because they feel that they are more your friend than not.

Grab a story of someone that they have in common with you or each other. Perhaps there is somebody that everyone in the audience is familiar with, like a group of students, a group of teachers, a community, a famous person that lives in the community. Make sure you get permission, but grabbing those stories and telling them as a connection to what it is that you really want to say is powerful.

A way that you add stories in your speaking is with the formula of *start a story* – content of speech – *finish the story*.

- When you are saying your story, you may not go through the entire story at one time. Instead try this: Start the story and get the audience interested. Then you drop in your content or your information that you need to share. Once you are done giving the content, you finish up the story on the back end. The audience will see all the connections.

- A lot of times when you tell the story, you may not need to explain why that story connects with the content and the information that you needed to share. Sometimes you do, but many times you don't. There are times that if it is a strong enough story, people will get it. You will look into the crowd, see the head nods, see the smiles. You will see the eyes squinting, all giving you confirmation that the story connected well with the content and outcomes that you were working toward.
- Consider having a twist or a shock in the story. If it is a story that has a twist or shock in it, build up to that twist. Use the same formula as before where you are sharing this story. Provide content. Then after the content you provide the finished or the shocking twist to that story. Another option is to give the shock, then give your content, and then wrapping up the story after the content shows how everything worked out okay in the end.
- Share a story and then share the lesson learned from that story. Provide your content and then finish the story.

There are many ways that you can use this. The whole purpose of using stories is to connect with others. People love to hear stories. They like to witness stories. They want to feel like they are familiar with the characters in the stories. Each person in the audience that listens to the story has an image of what the characters look like and what the characters are doing. That is what makes stories so strong.

Stories are the currency of human contact.
#standtallstatement

7.1.4. Connect with Your Audience

There are two ways that you can connect with your audience. You can connect with them intellectually or emotionally.

Intellectual connectivity makes you think.

Emotional connectivity makes you act.

As a Stand Tall Leader, most of the time when you are speaking or addressing a group of people, you want them to act. You want them to do something based on what you are saying. That action may be that you want them to think or ponder over things. Usually you want them to act on doing something because of what was said. Therefore, you need to connect with them intellectually and emotionally. Connecting emotionally is the most important way of making sure that people do take action. Connecting emotionally moves people out of compliance and closer to commitment. This can be done mostly by making eye contact. Make eye contact with those in the audience – everyone from the front rows to the back rows. Be sure to connect your eyes as with as many people as possible. Don't forget the sides and back of the room, not just the front middle. Connecting with them for half a second or two means so much. This is a very basic skill that we tell students to do all the time, yet we forget the value of doing this consistently.

Stand Tall Action

Be aware of the I/You ratio within your speech. What do I mean by the I/You ratio? Everyone is more interested in themselves than you. Be careful of how many times you are saying I *I* as opposed to saying *you* or referencing *others*. The people want to know what it is that you are saying and how relates to them. How is this story connected with my situation? Try to reduce these I-statements so that it is not all about you but it's about them.

When making a point or to get reassurance, it's okay to look at one or two people near the front as if you're talking to them as friends. Let's say that you are telling a story and as you tell the story you start to make your main point. Looking at the first two or three people in the middle or the front side and leaning into them, pointing to them or gesturing toward them for certain important parts of the story makes them feel like you are talking right to them. The audience may think, "Who is that? That could be me. Wow she's connecting deeply. She's connecting directly with us!" Then you pull back and you explain to everyone all the different important pieces of what it is that you said to the one or two people near the front. Your voice is still loud enough for everyone to hear and it is not a secret. Now *that* is connecting with the audience! They see that you care. They see that you mean what it is that you say. Simple little actions like making purposeful eye contact, looking directly at people, and gesturing to certain people builds that trust within the audience.

7.1.4.1. What's Up with Your Vocabulary?

We are in education. We have a certain set of words and vernacular that we are used to saying and use on a regular basis. Throwing out these vernaculars and terms that are very common in the world of education is easy to do. But people who are not in the world of education don't know it. It does not make you look smarter. It kind of makes you look like a snob. Don't talk down to people. Just use common language and vernacular that does not have to be deciphered with a dictionary. There is no need for the use of every acronym within education for one speech.

Instead of saying, "Through the standards that we utilized from the state assessment, we will differentiate all of our instruction through the IEP and the 504 process, which allows for systematic student PGs to the overall learning the students that was brought before the I&RS team we have within our, co-curricular learning establishment."

Just say, "We used the data from the state tests to help us plan better instruction for our students. We have some classrooms that are co-taught so that we can allow the students to create personal goals and the opportunity to get as much necessary instructional assistance as possible."

That makes more sense than all the extra educational vocabulary. That allows you to connect more with your audience and don't look like a snob.

7.1.5. Your Last Words Linger

A great quote by Patricia Fripp, who is a world-renowned speech writer, coach, and consultant states, "*Your last words linger*." Never think that what you say at the end of a speech doesn't mean something. They may forget a lot of what it is that you said throughout the speech, but the last few things and statements that come out of your mouth, will stay with the audience once they leave. *Never thank people for their time at the end of your talk*. Everyone does that. "I want to thank you for your time for coming here." No one is listening to that. As soon as they hear that, they start shutting their brains off, especially if you want to add a couple little things at the end of that statement. Different ways that you can close a speech or talk:

- Have a call to action. Have this audience do something. Challenge them to follow through. "I call upon you to do XYZ. . .," "I'm asking you to consider this. . ." "This is what we're going to do moving forward. . ." "Your job is. . ." There are many different ways that you can have a call to action. Now others are empowered based off of what it is that you said.
- If you're allowing questions from the audience, state it this way. "Before my closing remarks, are there any questions?" You want your closing remarks to be memorable? Don't end it with just the questions. You are leaving the ending up to chance. It could be that one community member who's going to question you and turn the tides of everything that you have said negative. Is that what you want everyone to know and feel when they leave your speech or talk? Therefore, let everyone know before your closing remarks, let's have questions. Be aware of your time. Be aware of the amount of space that you have so that

questions can be had and you are still able to have your closing remarks. Your last words linger when closing.

- Circle back to the start. You may need to go back to how you opened. Think of how you opened up your speech. What is it that you said? Was it a story? Was it a data? Was it a quote? Whatever it is that you did to start off your talk, loop back to that, restate that quote, finish the story that you started with in the beginning. Make sure that your last words linger in their mind by making your talk full circle.
- Some of you may remember the show *Colombo*. Colombo was a detective who had a unique way of getting the information for those he was questioning. One of the things that he would do after questioning someone is, he would start to walk away and then would turn around and say, "Oh, one more thing. . ." And then drop an additional little question or statement to them, which would turn the tide of everything that happened within that episode. Consider doing a Columbo close. Finish everything that you're going to say and then you say, ". . .before you go, one more thing. . ." Then state what it is that you want them to remember. State what your theme is. State the quote, refer to the story. Whatever needs to be done. Just do that extra little piece. It's like when you are writing a letter to someone and then at the bottom you put P.S. and a final little statement that gives you a nice little tagline.

Your last words linger. #standtallstatement

7.1.6. Index Cards Are Your Friend

When I create my speeches and try to figure out what I'm going to talk about, I go old-school style with index cards. This takes place well before the speech actually happens. Get yourself a stack of index cards. On the index cards you start to write concepts, thoughts, ideas, and stories. All the different things that make a speech interesting or concepts of what others may want to know. You put one concept on each index card. You are not looking to fill up the card front and back, but enough information that you are able to look at it and know what it is about. You may want to put some historical data, historical stories, some information about a personal story. Consider adding some information about the district, the school, some goals, some statements. This process doesn't happen at one time; it is collected over time.

When the time comes that you need to put together a speech or a talk, you can go to your card deck, find a large open table and start laying out the cards in columns in the order of how you want to say what needs to be said. The great thing about doing it this way is you are creating a storyboard. When creating new animations and stories for film, the people at Disney lay out a storyboard of how the story is to move forward. They use a big wall and bring people in to look at it. Because they laid out the storyboard, they can shift and move different parts of the story around. It's the same concept with planning your speaking. Once you have your cards in order. You can now start to practice and prepare.

Stand Tall Ideas

Pinning Ceremony

On the night that the incoming freshmen go for the orientation at one technology high school, they review what to expect. There are musical selections and students giving speeches about how they felt the first day of school and how they made it through. Following all the information and welcome speeches, all the new upcoming freshmen line up against the wall. Standing on the stage are the students who spoke, administrators, and a few teachers. Ten students at a time go up on stage, meet with the school representatives, and receive a pin with the school name on it. This pin represents their official admittance to the school. As the students are getting their pin, the parents are encouraged to take photos and there is fun music playing in the background. Following the pinning ceremony, there is a reception with refreshments and members from school clubs showcasing their club activities. The new freshmen are proudly wearing their new pins.

High-Five Wall

During your new student orientation, have students paint one hand and place the handprint on a designated wall. Have the students use a Sharpie marker to write their name under the handprint. Above the handprints paint a quote or the year of the class. Leave handprints on the wall until that class leaves/graduates from the school. Before leaving the school or walking out to graduation, have the students walk past the wall. I guarantee that each student will look for their hand and place their hand over it. It will be an emotion-filled moment for each student. As new students enter the class, make sure they get an opportunity to add their hand to the wall. As students leave the class, leave their hand up. It is a great remembrance for those who were with them throughout the years.

Prepare a backdrop or a scene as students enter into the school. Have the students take pictures of other students on their first day. Then post them on the in-house TV station, social media, or bulletin board in the school.

Welcome Back!

Have the mascot of the school at the entrance to welcome students and parents on the first day.

Give each teacher a free dress-down day pass to welcome them back to the start of the school year.

Give every staff member a T-shirt with the school theme. Wearing it on the first day showcases and supports the theme for the year.

Encourage staff with a dress-down day on the first day of school.

(*Continued*)

Send a survey out to all of the students to vote on the song that will be played on the first day of school as the students enter. This will build anticipation for the first day.

Send a *welcome back to school* letter to all of the students and take out all the letter U and R in the letter. At the end of the letter pose the question, "What is missing?"

Leave a welcome letter on each locker.

Using social media, have a countdown to the first day of school showing positive images of the school grounds.

WOW Committee

The WOW committee is a fun name for an interior decorating committee. Go out and recruit the teachers or students who have an eye for interior decorating or artistic flair. Meet together and start looking around the building for locations that do not look WOW. Basically, identify the locations in the school that do not seem very impressive. A good place to start is the main entrance. If possible, give the committee a small budget to work with and allow them to start decorating that area. You'll be surprised what they will come up with and do. It will completely change the look and the feel of your school. Allow the committee to decorate seasonally. Once the committee has decorated one area, allowing them to continue around the school to decorate other areas. The end result is a beautiful school that others take pride in. Another option would be to allow the committee to go into classrooms and decorate them for teachers if they so choose. The goal is for people to walk around your school and say WOW!

7.2. Parent Phone Communication

One of the things that educators are not always trained on is communicating on the phone with parents. Teachers, specifically, usually do not get formal training on how to do this. It is important that there is always positive communication when on the phone with parents. To be perfectly honest with you, most teachers have in the back of their mind a concern and worry for every single phone call. When they are about to talk to parents on the phone in the back of their mind, they are thinking, "Please don't yell at me. Please don't go off." Come on! You know this is true. I've spoken to educators around the country, and they have confirmed this continual concern and worry. As Stand Tall Leaders in the school, within our formal training, hopefully you have learned how to communicate with parents and some know how to have a positive phone call.

This understanding does not always translate down to the teacher level. Yet, as educational leaders we tell teachers to make parental phone calls. Then we give them a few tips here and there on how to survive a bad phone call. There are a few teachers, often the veteran teachers, who know exactly how to talk to parents. They know how to get through a tough call. And then there's the overall notion out there that teachers are never allowed to hang up on parents. Heaven forbid you ever do that! Yet it's okay to sit on the phone and get yelled at, screamed at, put down, and ridiculed. All of this also applies to us as school leaders.

Once as a building principal, I had a teacher make a positive phone call home. The teacher was planning to brag about the student to the parent. During the conversation, the parent had a concern about the student's learning that the teacher was unaware of. The parent brought it up immediately. The teacher started responding and getting a little defensive about what was being said by the parent. The parent got more defensive. The teacher got more defensive. Very quickly it turned into a horrible situation and a bad phone call. It got so bad that the teacher ended up hanging up on the parent mid-sentence. The parent called back then hung up on the teacher. It ended up getting to the vice principal level. It got to the principal level. It got to the assistant superintendent level. It got to the superintendent level. Eventually the parent showed up at the Board of Education meeting to complain about the teacher and school. It just got completely out of hand. The reason why it got out of hand is because of the teacher's response to the parent. Even though it was a veteran teacher who had dealt with parents for many years. Without proper training, it comes down to natural human instinct and wanting to defend herself and got very offended.

Because of this horrible interaction, I started to think very deeply about what it is that teachers needed in order to ensure that they have a positive conversation on the phone with parents. In doing so, I came up with a few things that needs to be focused on, specifically as it relates to talking to parents on the phone. This is good for teachers, administrators, and anyone who is talking on the phone.

7.2.1. Get Prepped

For every phone call you need to have the following:

- Notepad to take notes
- Calendar to be aware of your dates and times
- List of names and contact information of others in the school or district

Have a notepad so that you can take notes as to what is being said during the conversation. It does not matter if it is a good conversation or a bad conversation, have the notepad. You may think that you have a great memory, but as you are going through the conversation and you want to highlight specific areas, it is important to write them down and then refer back to them. It makes you seem less impulsive and more alert. It allows you to be a little smarter on the phone calls, so you know exactly what was said. If the phone call goes in a poor direction, now you have the notes of what exactly happened during that conversation.

Having a calendar to be aware of your dates and times is also very important as the conversation moves forward. Maybe you need to schedule a follow-up conversation. Instead of putting the parent on hold and looking for your calendar or trying to remember what you have going on, you now have your calendar right in front of you. Easy reference.

Maybe you are not going to solve what the concern is on the phone and you need to have a face-to-face conversation. You have your calendar right in front of you. You can easily review it and quickly show that you are ready to go.

Having a list of names of contacts and information of others in the district or the school is also very important. Let's say that the conversation gets to a point where you cannot solve the problem, or you do not have the answer. You need a quick list of names of people that you can refer the parent to. Instead of putting them on hold and saying, "Let me see if I can find the name and number/email," you have it right there with you. You confidently say, "Yes, I know exactly who you need to talk to. I have their contact information. Let me know when you are ready." You sound more professional. You seem ready at that moment instead of putting parents on hold and scrambling around and maybe you'll find the list and maybe you won't.

7.2.2. Shut Up

A lot of times, on the phone, especially as educators, we want to get right to what we need to say. We bombard the conversation so that our time is not wasted, and we tend to bully the parent through the call to stick directly to the points that we want to say. Let the parents talk through the concern or issue first. Just let them get through it. Many times, the parents just want someone to listen to them. There have been multiple times that I have been on the phone with parents who have a concern. I stopped talking and allowed them to "get it all out." Once they did that, I just paraphrased what they just told me, and the parent was satisfied. They didn't need a follow-up appointment, steps for engagement, or my opinion. They appreciated that I just shut up and listened. On multiple occasions, the parents said, "Thank you for listening; goodbye."

7.2.3. Write It Down

Write down the main points, the concerns, and issues that the parent is saying. Write down your talking points so you know what you want to say when it is your turn to talk, you will be ready to go. Don't worry too much about the word-for-word statements that were said by the parents. Get the big picture. Get the main points. Get the key words. As great as you think you are at multitasking, it's really not multitasking. You are just switching your focus from one action to the next quickly. If you write every word the parent says, you will not be able to be fully present within the phone call as much as you think.

7.2.4. Show Empathy

Showing empathy means that you are engaging with the conversation. They need to know that you are listening without agreeing with everything that has been said. As the parent is talking, you respond by saying statements like:

I see/Mmmm/Ahhh/Oh/Really?/Yes/Okay/Right/I hear you/Got it

Those types of statements reaffirm that you are listening. They do not indicate that you agree or that you do not agree. They simply state that you are listening. There should never be a time when a parent asks, "Are you still there?" Show that you're engaged in the conversation.

7.2.5. Take a Breath

If the parent is getting upset, you don't need to take it personally. Take a breath. Take a deep breath! Remain calm. Reaffirm yourself, "Okay, I got this." Pull the phone aside if you need to and gather yourself together. Take a deep breath. Meditate for a second. Do whatever you need to do to calm yourself down! The natural human instinct when someone starts yelling or being accusatory is to defend yourself. Seriously, what is that going to do at this moment? The other person is not in the frame of mind to listen. They are in the frame of mind to talk. Resist the urge to go back to the parent on the phone. Instead, take a breath, take your notes, and let them know you are listening.

7.2.6. Repeat What Was Said

Once you have all the information from the parent, you need to make sure that you repeat what was said back to the parent in your own words. Simply repeating back what the parent said clarifies what their concern is. There have been many situations as an administrator where I have simply repeated back to the parent what it is that they said and the parent responds back by saying, "Thank you so much. You truly understand what I'm concerned about. Goodbye," and they hang up the phone. They just needed somebody to listen to them and say that they understood what the concern is. Simply paraphrasing back to the parent what it is that they said allows them to know that you are listening and reaffirms that you understand.

After the situation with the teacher having the horrible phone call with the parent and it got to the principle level, superintendent level, and the board of education level, I created a list of things that needed to be focused on during parent phone conversations. I also created the *Parent Phone Call Flowchart*. The Parent Phone Call Flowchart outlines specifically how a teacher or anyone in education is to interact with parents on the phone without giving them specific wording of what to say.

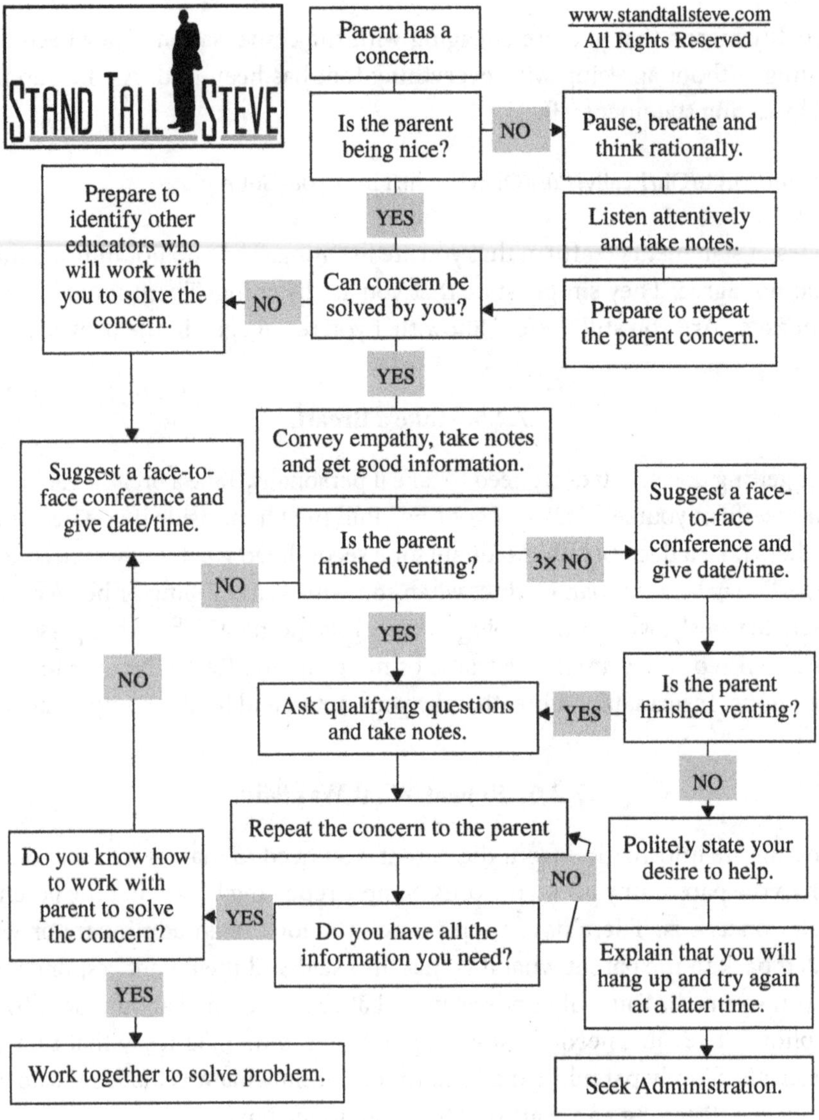

Looking at the Parent Phone Call Flowchart, let's review. It starts with the parent has a concern. At any time during the conversation if the parent has a concern that comes up, you moved to this spot.

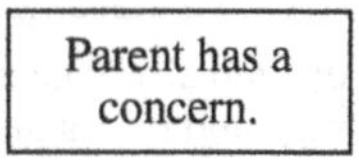

Next, *Is the parent being nice?* Yes or no? It's a very simple question. If the parent is saying what it is, they're concerned about in a nice way, well then you have nothing to worry about. Let's say the parent is not being nice at that point; now you know which direction to go. Let's go through this as if everything is going well: *Is the parent being nice?* Yes. *Can the concern be solved by you?* Not every situation is brought before the teacher can be solved by the teacher. A lot of times you listen to what's being said by the parent and then instantly you go into response mode.

You need to think. Can it be solved by you or can it not be solved by you? Sometimes certain things need to be solved by somebody else. It is not for you to do. For example, if you are an elementary teacher and something happened on the playground and you were not there. You are not aware of it, but yet you know that the outside playground supervisor was aware of it. Then you move over to *Prepare to identify other educators who will work with you to solve the concern.* This is why you have a list of names and contact information of other people in the school or district. Look closer. Notice it says, prepare to identify other educators who will *work with you*. If it is your child in your room, in your class, or under your purview, you still have some level of responsibility.

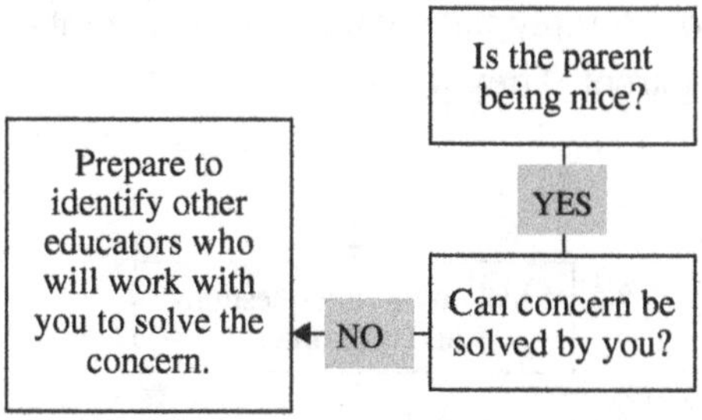

Everyone in the school should work together to support parent concerns. Every student belongs to everyone. Remember, you want *commitment* not just *compliance*. So, identify other people who will *work with you* to solve the issue or concern.

Let's say that the concern can be solved by you. *Convey empathy, take notes, get good information*. Again, conveying empathy means you respond to what it is that the parent is saying on the phone.

I see/Mmmm/Ahhh/Oh/Really?/Yes/Okay/Right/I hear you/Got it

Those statements are the things that reaffirms and makes the parent feel that you are listening. Make sure that you take good notes and get good information. Next, *Is the parent finished venting?* In this case, there is no venting. They are not upset. Everything is going well.

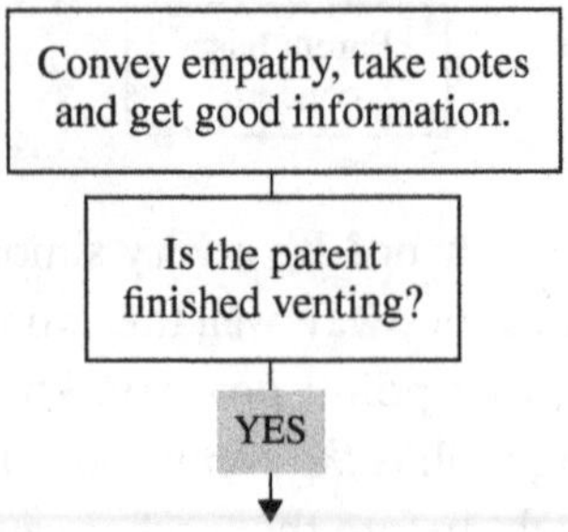

Next, *Ask qualifying questions and take notes.* Asking qualifying questions is important. You need to make sure that you got it right. Even if you know what the parent is saying perfectly, you should ask qualifying questions anyway! Why? Because that is what the parent needs to hear. They need to hear it in order to feel as if you truly understand what it is that they are talking about. Think back to when you were in college. There was that one student in class who would ask questions of the professor, but the way they would ask questions is they would simply repeat what the professor said in a form of a question. Everyone in class would roll their eyes and think, why would this person keep doing this? That person is a genius! That person gets it, because that is what you are going to do in this situation. No matter what. Even if you do not have a question, make up a qualifying question. Simply take what it is the parents said, turn it into a form or a question, and ask that to the parent. They will love it.

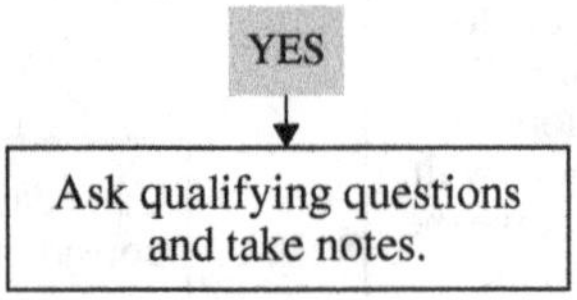

So, you have asked the qualifying question. You have taken additional notes. Next, you *Repeat the concern to the parent.* "So what you're telling me is. . ." If you don't have any qualifying questions, repeating the concern and the qualifying questions are the same. *Do you have all the information that you need?* Yes. *Do you know how to work with the parent to solve the concern?* Yes. *Work together to solve the problem.* Perfect.

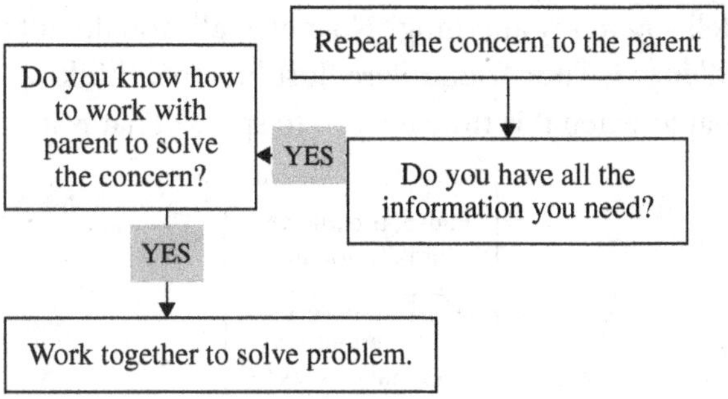

Now let's go through the *Parent Phone Call Flowchart* if the call does not go well. At any time during the progression of the call, the parents start to get upset and start to vent or go off on you, go back to the top of the form. *Parent has a concern. Is the parent being nice?* No! They're starting to get upset. Things are not working well.

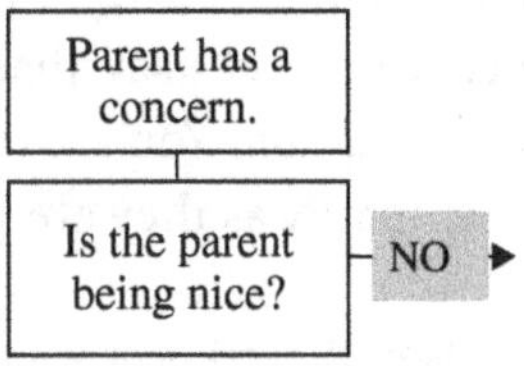

Pause, breathe, and think rationally. It is important that you take a breath. Breathe! Think about what it is that it's going on. Usually, when people get upset on the phone, you immediately start getting defensive. You want to start getting back at them for what it is they are saying to you. Rational thought starts to leave. You need to pause. Pull the phone aside, away from your mouth. If you have to take a deep breath, do it. Make sure that you are thinking rationally. Next, *Listen attentively and take notes.* At this point, it is most important that you take notes and listen carefully as to what is really being said, because a lot of times parents will say things that they regret, or they may speak in a way that is full of emotion. So, you need to listen to attentively as to what they really mean. Don't throw back into their face statements that they said specifically, which you know truly are not what they mean. Listen attentively and take notes about what it really means and then prepare to repeat the parent concern.

Remember to:

Pause, breathe, and think rationally.

Listen attentively and take notes.

Prepare to repeat the parent concern.

At any point, did I tell you to say anything? No, not at all. You do not say anything. Keep your mouth shut. Shut up! Silence is your friend here. Just breathe, think rationally, and listen. Take some notes and be prepared when it is time for you to speak. That is it.

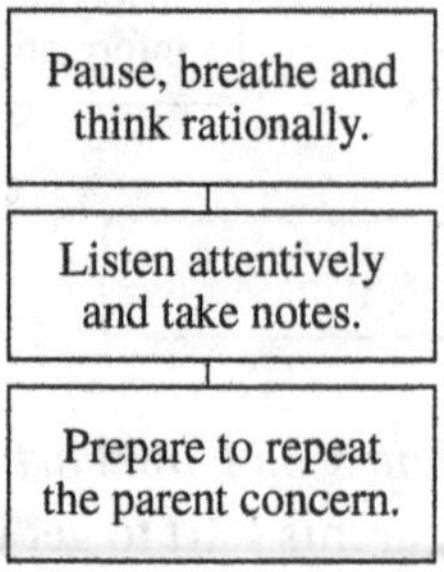

Can the concern be solved by you? In this case, maybe they are yelling and screaming about something that has nothing to do with you. If that is the case, *Prepare to identify other educators who will work with you to solve the concern.* Let's say that it is something that you can solve. *Convey empathy, take notes, get good information.* You are still not saying anything specifically. It is important to make sure you convey empathy as they are venting.

I see/Mmmm/Ahhh/Oh/Really?/Yes/Okay/Right/I hear you/Got it

If they are venting to you, say this specific statement, "Hold on, I'm writing that down." It is vitally important that you say that specific statement. When you say, "Hold on, I'm writing that down," what will the parent most likely do? They will most likely pause from the rant. Many times, when people suddenly stop from speaking loudly, they realize that they are speaking loudly. When they continue speaking, they will be less loud. It might not be that much less, but it will be less. It is important that you say specifically, "*Hold on. I'm writing that down.*"

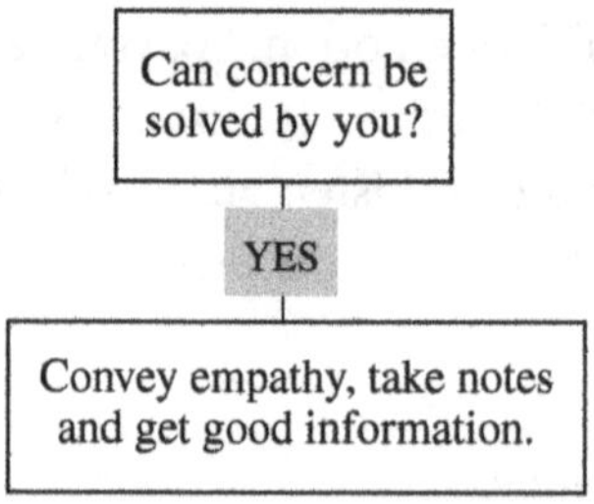

Is the parent finished venting? If you notice next to that statement it says 3x. Which means you are going to go through this process three times. If the parent is still venting after you have conveyed empathy, you have taken good notes, you have listened to them, they are still venting, you need to *Suggest a face-to-face conference and then give a date and time.* It does not do much good if you just say, I think we need to have a face-to-face conference and not give the date and time. That is why you always have your calendar in front of you. If the parent continues to vent, you pause, you listen a little bit longer, convey empathy. Then you state again, "I really think that we need to have a face to face conference. I'm available on Tuesday at 2:45 PM would that work?" If the parent is still venting a third time. You wait a little bit and you suggest a face-to-face conference once more. Give the date and time again. You have gone through the process of offering a time to meet three times. *Is the parent finished venting?* No, they are still going off at this point. You *Politely state your desire to help.* "Sir, I truly do want to help you with this situation." "Ma'am, I am here for your child and I would like to solve this issue and concern." You may have to interrupt them and say this. Then you will, Explain that you will hang up and try again at a later time. "Ma'am, I am now going to hang the phone up because this is not a productive conversation. Goodbye." Then you *HANG UP THE PHONE.*

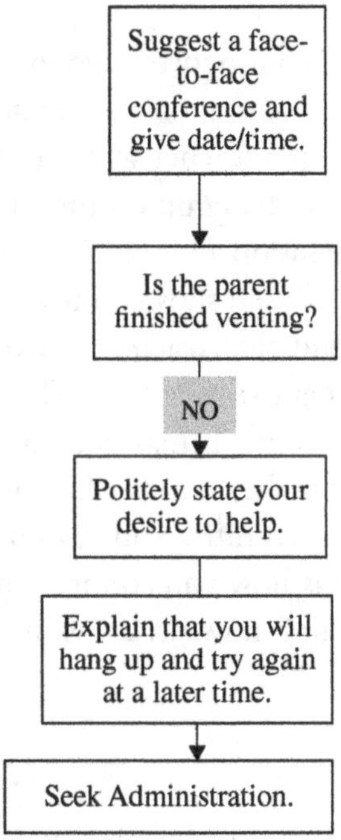

Did he just say hang up the phone? Yes. I said *hang up the phone.* You are a professional. You do not deserve to get yelled at, screamed at, put down, or ridiculed.

- You have offered them opportunities to have a face to face conference several times.
- You gave them a date and time.

- You conveyed empathy.
- You listened attentively.
- You provided notes.
- You asked qualifying questions.
- You did everything that it was necessary so that it would have a good outcome, but yet the parent continued to go off and vent.

Now, notice what it says at the very bottom *Seek Administration.* You just hung up on a parent! Obviously, you need to make sure that you go to administration and you let them know what has happened.

Seek Administration.

If you are the administrator, go to your network, go to a fellow administrator, talk it through. If you have a supervisor, reach out to them. If you are a teacher, find your school administrator. Let them know. Here is the thing, if it is a teacher who had a horrible conversation on the phone with a parent and unfortunately had to hang up on their parents. The teacher ran down to the administrator's office after the conversation and said, "Oh my goodness, I had a horrible conversation with the parent, but I did this. . ." and showed the administrator this flowchart. Would the administrator be able to easily defend that teacher? I would say yes! This *Parent Phone Call Flowchart* does not tell the teacher what to say, but more how to respond and how to guide themselves through conversations with parents. It makes it easier for the administrator. It makes it easier for the teacher, and it actually makes it easier for the parent. The parents know that they are heard and are given plenty of opportunities and options to connect positively with teachers, administrators, and the school. This is how you connect and communicate with parents on the phone. It is professional, it is personal. It flows in a positive way and permits outcomes that you want. It works!

Stand Tall Action

Work together with other educators and practice using the Parent Phone Call Flowchart. Have one person be the parent and the other the educator. Practice if it is a good phone call and a bad phone call. The more you practice the better you will be.

Parent Phone Call Flowchart Must-Haves

Every Phone Call Should Have the Following:

- Notepad to take notes
- Calendar to be aware of dates and times
- List of names and contact information of others in the school/district

Stop Talking So Much!

Let the parents talk through the concern or issue first.

Show Empathy

Engage so they know you are listening without agreeing with everything that is said.

Write It Down

Write down the main points, concerns, and issues that the parent is saying.

Write down your talking points so you know what to say when it's your turn to talk.

Take a Breath

If the parent is getting upset and yelling, don't take it personally and take a deep breath to remain calm.

Repeat

Once you have all the information from the parent, repeat what they said back to them in your own words.

Contact Administration

If you have to end the conversation because of verbal abuse, make sure you contact administration right away.

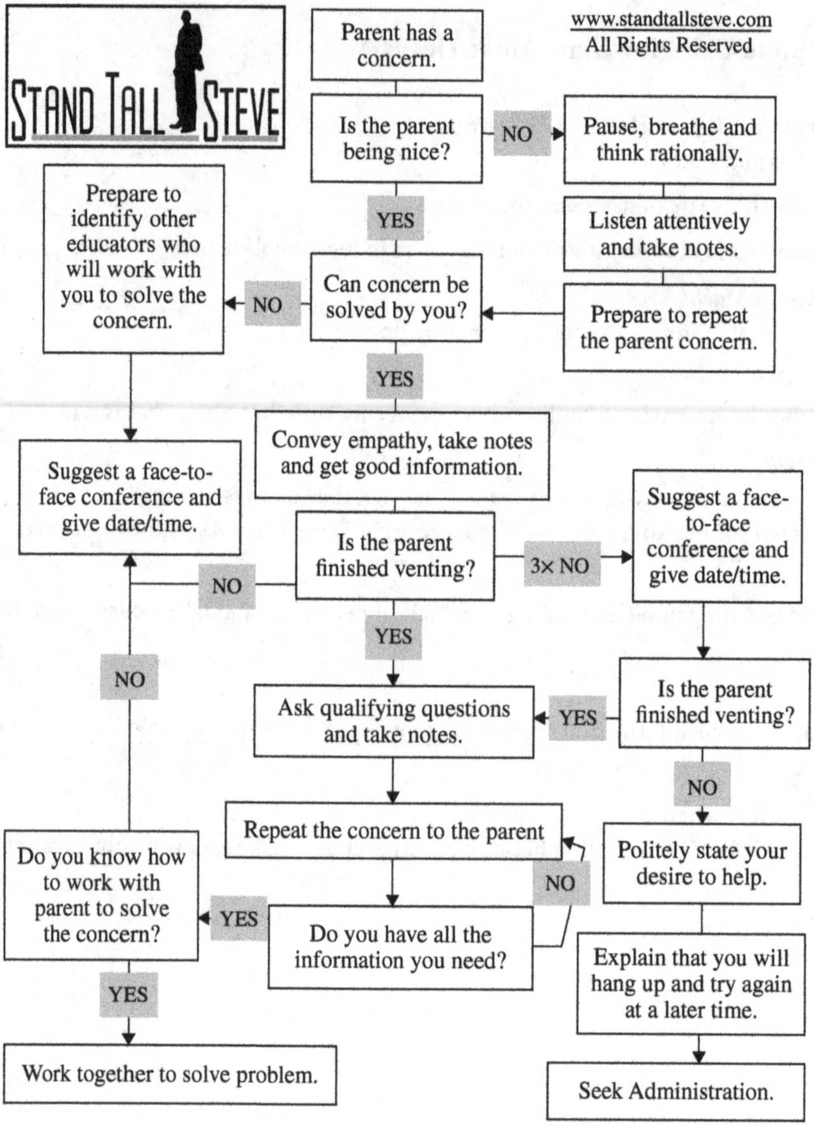
STAND TALL STEVE
www.standtallsteve.com
All Rights Reserved
Parent has a concern.
Is the parent being nice?
NO
Pause, breathe and think rationally.
Listen attentively and take notes.
Prepare to repeat the parent concern.
YES
Can concern be solved by you?
NO
Prepare to identify other educators who will work with you to solve the concern.
YES
Convey empathy, take notes and get good information.
Suggest a face-to-face conference and give date/time.
Is the parent finished venting?
3× NO
Suggest a face-to-face conference and give date/time.
NO
YES
NO
Ask qualifying questions and take notes.
YES
Is the parent finished venting?
NO
Repeat the concern to the parent
Politely state your desire to help.
NO
Do you know how to work with parent to solve the concern?
YES
Do you have all the information you need?
Explain that you will hang up and try again at a later time.
YES
Work together to solve problem.
Seek Administration.

Stand Tall Ideas

Back-to-School Night

Over the years, I have never outlined specifics for my teachers related to *back-to-school night*. For the most part, I have assumed that everyone knew what to do and did a good job. Nevertheless, I started to think about back-to-school night and what it means. Back-to-school night is a reputation builder. It is a time to make a great first impression. When your parents exit the room, you want them sold "hook, line, and sinker" to your teaching style, love of teaching, and methods. This is an opportunity to make "parent relationships" matter. Therefore, here are five things that I think are important to have to make back-to-school night matter.

Shake a Hand

Stand at the door and greet the parents as they enter. Similar to how you greet your students at the door when they come to your class. Most of the time, teachers hang in the classroom and await the parents. Teachers are a bit nervous and feel secure standing in the classroom. Trust me, greeting the parents before they enter the room alleviates a lot of that nervous energy. Additionally, it sets a great tone for your time together. Shaking hands and greeting at the door goes a long way in developing a positive relationship with parents.

Practice

Practice your presentation. In my school, the teachers have eight minutes per class period in order to present the material to the parents. Nothing gets you more off track than looking up at the clock and realizing that you only have one minute left and 10 more items to go over. At that point, you start apologizing to the parents, rushing through your material, blushing, and sounding unprofessional. Take the time to practice the presentation. Don't just review your notes. Stand in front of your room and do the full presentation. If possible, have a colleague watch your presentation and help you get it just right.

Something in Hand

Always offer a handout. The super parent and the mega difficult parent will have a notebook to take notes. Everyone else will most likely scribble information on the back of the schedule they have or do nothing at all. Providing a short half-page or full-page handout with your main points on it is very valuable to the parents. It is also beneficial to the parents who are late getting into your room and missed most of the presentation and are now holding you hostage into the late hours of the night. Remember, on each handout, make sure you have all of your contact information. This includes your phone, email, and best time to reach you.

(*Continued*)

Sign Here...
Make sure you have a sign-in sheet for parents or basic information card to fill out. On the sheet/card, have the following:

- Print name
- Sign name
- Phone number
- Email
- Best time to contact

By getting the above information, you will have clear evidence of what the parent signature looks like, quick access to their phone numbers, email, and when to call and hold a conversation if needed.

Vocabulary
Be cognizant of the language you use when speaking to parents. Within each industry, there is a vocabulary and vernacular that is used. We cannot expect our parents to know all of the words and terminology that we use on a daily basis. Using phrases like, ". . .consistent differentiation through conferencing and instructing within the constructivist method. . ." does not make you sound smart. Basically, you sound like you are not in touch with the students and a bit of a snob. Use simple everyday language. Slow. . . it. . . down. When people are nervous, they tend to speed up their talking. Talking fast confuses the parents and leads to them asking questions to clarify what you said. Keep it simple.

Teacher Trivia
In the parent newsletter, slip in some trivia about the teachers who work at the school. You can even write an article highlighting specific new teachers in the school. This allows the community and parents to make a connection with the teachers that are in the school. A great twist to this is to send out a text or tweet to all of the parents with a question about the trivia of the teacher, and the parent who can return that information first or second gets a prize. After doing that a few times, you will get parents reading the newsletter more often and the connections become even stronger.

7.3. Uncomfortable Silence

There are times that I walk into situations where I meet a person or a group of people who met me for the first time. Many times when that happens, I get the same looks. They do their best not to show that they are staring at me or wondering the obvious questions. How tall am I? Do I play basketball? Eventually, somebody will say, wow, you are tall. As if I did not know this already. Once they ask how tall I am, I give them an answer or I ask, what do you think? Most of the time I just tell them that I am six foot seven and, no, I do not play basketball. Yes, I played in high school, blah, blah, blah. After I answered the questions, usually there is a moment of silence. That moment of silence is uncomfortable. That uncomfortable moment of silence is when the person is processing what I said. They don't have a comeback because the response that I gave them isn't what they were expecting. So it gets a little weird.

At that moment, in the past I would feel it necessary to fill in that empty silence with either another joke or something else just so it would not feel awkward. Over time I started to realize that it's not my empty silence to own. It is theirs. They are the one who posed the question. They are the one who needs to think and process. They are the one who needs to understand what I said. Therefore, I started the practice of being comfortable with uncomfortable silence.

During that little bit of uncomfortable silence, I realized that they need that time to process and they need to understand that they have to respond back to me – hopefully in a way that won't make them look silly. Unfortunately, usually they say something that does. That moment of uncomfortable silence is processing time. It's time for them to truly think about what it is that they said, how I responded, and what the next step would be.

I've taken this moment of silence and being comfortable with uncomfortable silence into my leadership. As a Stand Tall Leader, there are times that you want others that are working under you to process what it is that you have said, to get an understanding of what needs to be done. Many times people expect others to come up with an answer right away. Have the right thing to say all the time. Life is not a sitcom where you always have the best witty response or the perfect answer every time. It doesn't work that way. We don't have a team of writers behind us that help us come up with the right statements and a director to show us how to say it the right way. People need time to process. So, therefore, as a Stand Tall Leader, when you are working with other staff members, parents, or students, just wait.

People need to have that processing time, that empty space where it is silent. Either they don't want to respond, they don't want to engage their minds to start thinking or they know what to say, but they are worried about what others think. That is valuable. As a leader, you need to not interrupt that uncomfortable silence in that processing time so that they can do what they need to do. In turn, you grow as a leader.

We as leaders have the answers. We know exactly what needs to be said. A great leader doesn't always know the answer, and they are waiting to see what others are going to say so that they can continue the learning and process. You need to get comfortable with uncomfortable silence. You need to allow others the opportunity to think through what it is they need to think through and to be able to do. Within the *five levels of decision-making*, being comfortable with uncomfortable silence is key for levels 3 and 4. Those levels are designed specifically for you the leader to say your piece and then shut up. Others need time to process what you say and then act on it.

When I speak and provide training to schools and educators around the country, at times I ask the audience to respond or discuss openly a topic or concept. I come right out and say to everyone in the audience, "Just so you know, I am very comfortable with uncomfortable silence." Usually, I get a few chuckles and laughs, but then I stand there silently, and they start to realize, "Oh my goodness, he really is going to be silent!" Usually, this is how it works. I make a statement. They chuckle, they laugh, and then one second goes by, two seconds go by. After about two seconds, they start to realize, oh wait, I need to start thinking, and after three or four seconds, wait a second, what is it that he said? Okay, that's right. Now what do I think about that? Five seconds go by. Oh, now it's starting to get uncomfortable. You can feel it around you. The environment, all the sudden changes. All I do is stand there and I look around with a big smile. I don't say a word. I don't prompt them. Nothing.

Keep in mind, usually when you are talking with other adults in education, they are smart. They are not idiots. They can formulate an answer. You think that you need to coax them along or try to help them? They made it through high school, most made it through college. If they were able to get through that, why shouldn't they be able to get through your question? So usually around the six-second time slot, someone raises their hand or says something. When that happens, you can usually respond by saying, thank you very much for breaking the uncomfortable silence, and they chuckle. As soon as you say that, it lessens that tension in the room. Then the process starts over again. But usually the amount of uncomfortable silence shrinks a little bit more, a little bit more, a little bit more. Understand that as a tall person, uncomfortable silence is always there. Use that uncomfortable silence to your advantage. Think of ways that you can continue the learning. Allow people to struggle a little bit. In the struggle is where the learning takes place the most. Get comfortable with uncomfortable silence.

When Can Uncomfortable Silence Be Used?

- Faculty meetings
- Team meetings
- Pre and post observation meetings
- Parent meetings
- PTO/PTA meetings
- Professional development
- Disciplinary meetings
- Department meetings

Get comfortable with uncomfortable silence. #standtallstatement

Stand Tall Ideas

Leave a Message after the Beep. . .BEEP!

Many teachers now have a phone in their classroom, as well as an extension to call from and to receive messages. In most cases, the teacher's greeting sounds something like this: "This is Mr. Smith's extension. I am not available. Please leave a message after the beep and I will get back to you within 24 hours." That is a typical answer that everyone expects and can be the start of a series of exchanged messages. Look at a voice mail message as an opportunity to share information with whoever is calling, both to provide a better experience for the parent and to save the teacher time and frustration. Consider adding these to a voice mail greeting:

- The room number of the classroom
- The best time to reach you during your prep hour
- The extension of the main office
- The school motto or theme
- Your email addresses

If possible, record a new message daily or weekly that includes:

- Explanation of the next test or quiz with the day and time
- Homework assignment for the night/week

You can change the message daily, weekly, monthly, or yearly. The goal is to provide information beyond leaving a basic message. Trust me, it goes a long way.

Turn Up Tenure

If you are a tenured teacher or administrator, think back to the day you got tenure. I am sure it was filled with excitement, joy, and celebration. The many gifts and congratulations were overflowing. You could barely contain the excitement. NOT!

For most of us, the day we got tenure was like any other day of work. Yes, a few people may have said congratulations. Possibly you got a plant from the union. A select few got a handshake from an administrator.

I challenge you to think of tenure as a milestone and powerful right of passage. Getting tenure states that as a school, as a district, and as a community we trust you. We feel that you are able to instruct the children to the level we expect. It states that you've got the "Right Stuff"! Therefore, when someone gets tenure it should be celebrated and recognized appropriately. Here are four ways to recognize your tenure staff.

(*Continued*)

Tea, Anyone?
Have a tenure tea. Invite the staff that has obtained tenure to a special tea or lunch. Taking the time to break bread together and express how important they are to the school community goes a long way. The tea or lunch can be in school or out at a local restaurant. Possibly even connect with the restaurant to get a discounted meal and have a special sign at the reserved table saying congratulations.

In the News
Contact the local paper and run an ad showcasing the tenured teachers. Use "CONGRATULATIONS" as the headline with the names underneath. Don't forget to show the names on the school marquee, bulletin boards, school newsletter, school website, school Facebook page, and Twitter. The focus is to show everyone how important it is to get tenure in your district.

Just for You
Go to your local embroidery store and get an item embroidered with the tenured teacher's name on it. Having a special item that signifies this event will mean a great deal to each educator who gets one. Many items can be personalized:

- Pen
- Trophy
- Glass apple
- Desk sign
- Plaque
- Letterman jacket
- Superman cape
- School bell
- Mascot ornament
- Class ring

Some great websites for personalized gifts: www.personalizationmall.com, www.personalcreations.com, www.thingsremembered.com

Come See Me
If you are an administrator, take the time to meet with each tenured staff on the day they get tenure. Make sure the meeting is private with no interruptions. Explain why you hired him/her. Share some funny stores that you both can reminisce about. Outline your future expectations and say how proud you are to be working with him/her. This meeting will be burned into the educator's

memory. It is an important opportunity to solidify the administrator/educator relationship for the future.

The purpose of recognizing your tenured staff is more than making each tenured person feel good. It is about sending a clear message that every person in the school is valued and plays an important role. It tells the community that you value your staff and "We don't just let anyone teach our kids." It bonds and strengthens the relationships within the school. Take the time to make the tenured experience meaningful.

CHAPTER › EIGHT
Stand Tall Leaders Are Reflective

8.1. Hold on a Second

As a Stand Tall Leader, you must always be aware of your presence and how other see you. As you know, you are always on display. Everyone is watching what you do and what you don't do. There are very few times that you are not being watched, listened to, or modeled. With this understanding, it is important that you are selective, specific, and focused with your words, actions, and decisions. I am sure that have been times that you have said, did or decided something quickly and soon realized that, oops, you acted too quickly. Now you have to back up, clarify your statement, or change your direction. As a Stand Tall Reflective Leader, you need to hold on a second from time to time.

8.1.1. Three Levels of Decision-Making

Earlier we learned about the *five levels of decision-making*. The five levels are a way to make decisions that provide clear direction to you and others about how decisions are made as well as providing opportunities for others to be empowered. This process is most useful and powerful when others know what level you are using specifically.

Level one is reserved to you the leader. You make a decision without anyones input. It is usually reserved for emergency events or when time is a factor so that a solution becomes reality quickly. When it comes to holding on a second, level 1 decision-making isn't the way to go. However, the next three levels are perfect for you to hold on a second before making a decision. Level 2 is when you make a decision after you get input from others. Once you have gotten the input from others and gathered the information that you need, this is a great opportunity to pause and make eye contact before making your decision. Even if you already know what you are going to say, *hold on a second*. During that second of time, you are waiting to make eye contact with whoever else is in the room. That second of making eye contact is HUGE! It portrays to others that you are thinking of them, not yourself. You may think that holding your head down, to the side or seeming like you are thinking would be beneficial. It might be, but not as much as two seconds of eye contact. Those two seconds of eye contact strengthen your following statement. That can make all the difference in whether others will take the decision that was said and agree with it. For some, those two seconds of eye contact will move them from *compliance* to *commitment*. Just hold on a second and reflect before giving your decision.

This technique is equally valuable for levels 3 and 4. Remember, level 3 is you all make a decision together equally. Level 4 is when you give your feedback and then they make a decision. In both situations, holding on a second to reflect and provide eye contact will strengthen what you have to say.

Within level 3, others will know that you care and are thinking of others with your input and decision. They will in turn do the same thing. They will also *hold on a second* and reflect just a bit longer with their decision before sharing with the group. The probability of others being more committed to the decision becomes higher when reflection takes place.

Within level 4 you pause and give eye contact before sharing your thoughts. This will allow those who are making the decision to have a sense that you truly care and want the best from them when they are making the decision.

Hold on a second before making a decision. #standtallstatement

A two-second pause with eye contact is a powerful thing. This short moment of reflection will set the tone and direction within the three levels of decision-making.

8.1.2. Pause Before You Post

I really shouldn't have to state this, but I just have to make sure that I do. Because of the world we live in, it is extremely important that we as leaders *Pause Before You Post* anything electronically. Just to be transparent, I did not come up with the term *Pause Before You Post*. Pause Before You Post is a trademarked program sponsored by Jostens for students to think before posting on social media. Even though it is directly designed for students, it is relevant to everyone. Specifically, Stand Tall Leaders.

As you know, Stand Tall Leaders don't blend in and are seen at all times. This is true in the physical world and also in the electronic world. I remember there were times that I would think that nobody was reading my emails. When posting something on social media, maybe no one would comment or "like" it. Maybe I had no followers. I would think, I might as well just be talking to myself. After all, I have to repeat myself constantly regarding what I put in the email. I would send a second and third email out with the first sentence stating, . . . per my previous email. . . I'm thinking there is no way I'm Standing Tall within my electronic communication. Then I would make a typo, or little misstate within one email. The floodgates would open with multiple people pointing out the mistake. This is overwhelming evidence that I am definitely a Stand Tall Leader within my electronic communication.

When communicating electronically, make sure that it is in alignment with what you respect and value. Reinforcement of what you respect and value comes through your electronic communication loud and clear:

- Your electronic communication can be a main source of internal branding you have to promote how you will lead.
- Your electronic communication can be a main source of strengthening your behavioral culture and scheduled culture.

- Your electronic communication can be a main source of maintaining your climate from hour to hour, day to day, week to week, etc.
- Your electronic communication can be a main source to move people from compliance to commitment.
- Your electronic communication can be a main source to share your levels of decision-making.
- Your electronic communication can be a main source of differentiating between effectiveness and efficiency.

Knowing this, it would make sense to be very reflective when it comes to your electronic communication and *pause before you post.* Take a moment and read through what it is you wrote. Does it truly express what it is that you want? Can it be misinterpreted? What is your emotional state when writing it? Do you need to let someone else read it first?

Keep in mind that a Stand Tall Leader does not blend in within the physical world and electronic world. Take a minute to reflect and pause before you post.

A Stand Tall Leader does not blend in within the physical or electronic worlds. #standtallstatement

8.2. Stand Tall Professional Development

I have to admit. It can be difficult to find quality professional development (PD) as a Stand Tall Leader. I find it amazing that within the world of educational leadership there are so few opportunities for high-level PD that is easily accessible and meaningful to what we do on a regular basis. In order to be a Stand Tall Leader, it is important that you continually work to make yourself better and strengthen your level of influence.

Over the years, I have found that in order to get the very best training and leadership development, I may have to expand beyond the normal PD mail flyers and email advertisements. Thinking differently about PD and the different formats it comes in will allow you to have more options with growth, reflection, and development.

8.2.1. Books

Obviously, books are an excellent way to grow and learn. If you didn't believe that you wouldn't be reading this right now. I have found a wide variety of books that have elevated my learning, improved my influence as a leader. As many educational leader books that I have read, I read twice as many self-help and leadership books. We are in the business of working with people. We need to make sure that we are influencing people toward what we respect and value. Therefore, it makes sense to me to read books about how to do that best. Finding ways to move people toward outcomes. Empower people to become better. Strategies to speak better and plan more effectively. A more balanced life. Develop meaningful relationships. Basically, if I am a better person, I'll be a better leader. Below are a few of my favorite books that have nothing to do with educational leadership, yet have everything to do with educational leadership:

- *How to Talk to Anyone,* by Leil Lowndes
- *Never Split the Difference,* by Chis Voss
- *Exactly What to Say,* by Phil M. Jones
- *Disney U,* by Doug Lipp
- *Get Sh*t Done,* by Jeffrey Gitomer
- *Play The Man,* by Mark Batterson
- *Great Leaders Have No Rules,* by Kevin Kruse
- *Creating Magic,* by Lee Cockerell
- *Just Listen,* by Mark Goulston
- *Made to Stick,* by Chip Heath and Dan Heath

8.2.2. Conferences

When attending a conference, this is what usually happens. You go to several breakout sessions and you learn some amazing things that can make an impact within your school and leadership. You possibly have 5–10 pages of notes. You may have even put stars or numbers next to some of the notes so that you know what to look back on. Then you go home and back to work. The notes are in a conference folder that you may or may not place on your desk. You goal is to go through the notes and pick a few things that you can start to implement. One week goes by. Two weeks go by. Three weeks go by. Eventually, two months go by and that folder with the amazing ideas in it is under a pile of other papers. You never got to doing anything from the conference.

It is important that you get something from that conference and implement it. You need to reflect on what was learned and make a plan to put it into action. Get an understanding of what the best ideas are and how long it will take to implement. Below is an outline of how you can do this. You MUST do this before you leave the conference. (See Stand Tall Conference Action Plan.)

Stand Tall Conference Action Plan

What do you respect in your school?

1. ______________________________

2. ______________________________

3. ______________________________

Top Ideas

Short Term	Mid Term	Long Term

Start by identifying what you respect in your school. This is a guide for you to make sure the ideas you select connect directly to that which is most important in your school.

Short Term: Write the ideas that you can do within the week.

Mid Term: Write the ideas that you can do within the next 3–4 months.

Long Term: Write the ideas that you can do next school year.

8.2.3. Mastermind Groups

What is a Mastermind Group? A Mastermind Group is a group of like-minded, committed people who meet regularly to share ideas, network, and support each other. This is a common practice within corporate areas and entrepreneurs. The Mastermind Group sets an agreed upon time to meet either face to face or via video conference. Usually, there is someone who hosts or maintains the agreed upon norms of the group. From there the host poses a question for discussion, and off you go. The group then discusses the topic, shares ideas, and asks others in the group for their opinion and help when needed. The outcome of the Mastermind group is the production of new ideas, new processes, problem solving, and comradery.

Mastermind Groups are a powerful way to provide yourself with quality PD on a weekly basis. Each week within the meeting time you will get the combined wisdom of everyone within the group. As school leaders you will have a strong support group who "get it." They will understand the struggles of the position and are committed to sharing solutions. I have found Mastermind Groups to be the very best personalized PD.

If you are interested in joining a Stand Tall Mastermind Group, visit http://www.standtallsteve/mastermind-group .

8.3. Standing Tall Words of Power

As you go through your time being a Stand Tall Leader, you need to be aware of what it is your community needs. There are a lot of different things that they need as it relates to quality, instruction, curriculum, good leadership, empowering environment. Along with all those things, there are some basic needs that you may want to ensure that everyone experience. It's almost like the basic human rights or basic human needs of every human. These are things that students and staff alike need to be aware of and feel. If you use these as an underlying current for your leadership, for your school environment, for your district environment, you will be able to provide so much more than just a basic leadership. Even though these are basic words they are words that everyone in your school wants in their life or manifested in the environment and the actions of those around them.

8.3.1. Love

Love is the foundation of all human needs. It does not matter your race, culture, or ethnicity. Everyone wants it. Everyone needs it. Not everyone accepts love the same way. There's a wonderful book called *The Five Love Languages* by Gary Chapman. Five love languages focus on how people give love and receive love. The goal is understanding not only how love is given but how it is received. How it is received means so much more. Many times when you show love in the love language of someone else, it can be a struggle. Especially if that is not be the way that you show love. Regardless, it is important that it is shown. Five love languages revolve around acts of service, time, gifts, touch, and words of affirmation. Looking at those five different love languages, you have to make sure that they are portrayed and given throughout the school and throughout the district. Just as there are different learning styles, there are many different love styles. Think about ways to show it so that everyone feels loved.

8.3.2. Acceptance

We all want to be accepted by others. People do crazy things to be accepted by other people. They eat things that they shouldn't eat. They drink things they shouldn't drink. They have relations with people they shouldn't have relations with. All for the need for acceptance of those around them. There are YouTube channels and videos of people doing all kinds of different things in order to get a thumbs up or get the acceptance from other people. For us as Stand Tall Leaders, we need to make sure that we are developing an environment where acceptance is the norm. Showcasing students and staff abilities and promoting the good they do. It needs to be a full-on internal branding as it relates to acceptance of others. Do not hope that it happens. Hope is not a plan. Make it happen. Be purposeful in your planning and daily actions to develop events, statements, and actions that support continual acceptance of all groups within the school.

8.3.3. Wanted

It is one thing to be accepted, but it's another thing to be wanted. Want is the desire to have you there. If someone is accepted, they just so happen to be there, and others are okay with them being in the space. Being wanted means that you have been sought out. Being sought out for what you can bring to the table and who you are. There are tons of dating sites all focused around a desire to be wanted. They put out their very best, and they see who is swiping right and swiping left, because they want to feel that need of desire.

When you are wanted, you may perform better and do your very best beyond what is accepted. If somebody recruits you, you feel an obligation to showcase what you can do. Stating that you are seeking out specific people for their skills to help grow the school may build an allegiance to the school. Someone who is wanted will move closer toward commitment and out of just compliance.

8.3.4. Forgiveness

We all mess up. You know we all mess up. I think I messed up about 10 minutes before writing these sentences. Messing up is something that we all do, and we need to know that when we mess up, there is the possibility of forgiveness. Maintaining consequences is important. But you don't want your consequences to linger when the punishment is done. When it's done, it's done. Take the consequence for the actions of what was done and then let it be over. Saying that someone is forgiven is powerful. It is like a release. "I know what you have done, but now I honestly forgive you." You take the consequence; you take the punishment if it's necessary, and then move on. It's okay to fail. It's not okay to stay in failure.

It's okay to fail. It's not okay to stay in failure. #standtallstatement

Stand Tall Ideas

Heart to Heart Award

This award is for the staff only and involves an old bowling pin. It starts with giving the bowling pin to a teacher and explaining that at the next staff meeting he/she is to give the bowling pin to another teacher. At the start of the staff meeting, explain that a new award is starting. That teacher gets up and says something nice about the person he/she is giving it to and then hands the person the bowling pin award. That person is to hold the bowling pin for one month and then give the pin to another person who has made an impact in some way.

What is interesting is that as each person passes the pin on, it might gain a little more personality. One group added stickers, glasses, hair, and face. By the end of the school year, it didn't look like a bowling pin at all – it took on new meaning. This award became the most cherished award among the staff, because it came from the heart.

This Bud's for You

This idea is a great way to start a faculty meeting. Prior to the faculty meeting, place some flowers next to the meeting sign-in sheet. Once everyone arrives and sits down, whoever took a flower can stand up and thank a fellow staff member for whatever they want, then give the flower to the other staff member. This is a feel-good opportunity for the staff to thank each other for the great things they do every day. It publicly acknowledges each other and supports positive relationships. Do this at every meeting and you are starting the meeting with positive vibes and warm fuzziness.

Bulletin Board Award

If you are in a school with bulletin boards, you know how shabby some boards can be. Additionally, the boards tend to remain the same all year long. A great way to encourage staff to spruce them up is to have a monthly or quarterly Bulletin Board Award. Make sure you have groups or people assigned to the bulletin board throughout the year. Select the dates for completion of the boards and the judging. Use the custodial staff as judges – I did this and the custodial staff loved it! They reminded the groups when the boards were due and made sure the groups got supplies, they needed to make the boards great. They asked questions about the reason for the boards and even praised the students who had work on the board or worked on the board. The prize was an announcement to the entire school body and a blue ribbon was put on the board. At one point the custodial staff wanted to make the announcement to the school and made a certificate for the winners.

8.4. Three Sides of Leadership Growth

Three actions can make a leader more rounded in their ability to lead and learn. They are so important that anyone who wants to excel in any area needs to make them a part of their leadership philosophy. These three areas will allow a leader to have the fullness of the leadership experience. Let's explain each one of these.

Mentor someone in leadership.

Connect with someone else who leads.

Be mentored by someone who leads.

8.4.1. Mentor Someone in Leadership

Obviously, you would not be a leader unless you have someone that you are leading. But in this case, we are looking at it more personally than just having a staff or a district that you lead. You need to have a mentee, someone that you are helping to move along the leadership continuum. Have someone who may aspire to be like you, a leader.

Remember where we are in the world of education. We are educators. No matter what level we sit in, we are all in the business of educating. Even if it feels like you are drowning in the sea of administrivia and it seems that you are losing sight of the leadership you provide. Remember, this is all about learning. It is important that you identify others who would like to aspire to be better within leadership. It doesn't matter if it is your first year in administration or your 40th year. There is something that you can share with someone else. People are at many different levels within their growth. It could be one person, or it could be a few people. The goal is to identify, connect, and start setting the example. You will be spreading your knowledge to others so that they can take what they learn from you and place it in their own lives. You are a cheerleader for them. You are providing opportunities for them to grow.

Finding the right person or people to do this may take time. Sometimes you find the person and sometimes the person finds you. I get it, I get it, you want to help a lot of different people. Yes, you want to connect with a lot of people. Yes, you want them to live better in their lives, but having those specific individuals that you take the time out to truly help give your information and give your knowledge to provide opportunities for is special. Think back to when you were starting your journey toward leadership. Did you have someone you looked up to? Did you have someone who mentored and guided you? At one point were you searching for the person to answer the questions you had? You can be that person for someone else.

You may be wondering if others are going to be concerned about you playing favorites. I never said that the person would be someone who works directly with you. It could be someone from another school or district. A different town or across the country. With the benefits of technology and communication, it is easier to develop and maintain the mentor mentee relationship. It is vitally important as a leader to continually have that relationship so that you could have that fulfillment of helping others move up and do well. Make it purposeful.

By chance has there ever been a time you have made an impact on someone's life? or someone has watched you and has learned so much from you. Then one day they told you what you did to impact their lives. I am sure you were thinking, "I didn't know. I was just being myself." Followed by the thoughts of, "I want to help them more." At this point that person is like a little project. When the time comes when you have gotten them to where it is that they need to be, reflect on the relationship and what was learned. I am positive that you will have learned just as much, if not more, than your mentee.

8.4.2. Connect with Someone Else Who Leads

You need to have a network of other leaders who think like you or at least think a little differently than you, but who understand your circumstance. Within that network you can share experiences as a leader. One thing I learned early in my leadership is that leadership in education is lonely. Even though you cannot blend in and everyone knows you, the position you are in is lonely. Many times you may be the only one like you in the building. You do not always have a large network of others around you that you can share your ideas and thoughts with. You are not able to drop ideas and get a different opinion from others often. There is no common planning time in educational leadership. This level of loneliness at times causes you to second guess yourself and leads to administrator guilt.

That is why it is important to be a part of a leadership association. Don't just be a part of the association but get directly involved with the association. The goal is to connect, network, and share ideas with other educators. An association is the closest thing you can get to a common planning time for educational leaders. I speak at many educational associations throughout the country. Two specific associations that have developed a very strong supporting environment with is the Missouri Association of Elementary School Principals (MAESP) and Kentucky Association of School Administrators (KASA). Each of these associations provide conferences and opportunities for their membership to network and take care of each other. Not only do they talk about legislation and making an impact on educational leadership, but they have a Culture of taking care of each other and making meaningful connections so that administrators do not feel alone.

One of the things about tall people that many people don't know is that there are tall people, groups, associations, and memberships where tall people get together with each other. You may think, "That's kind of funny to look at a bunch of tall people standing around laughing and joking." Or you may think, "I've heard of a tall person association; it's called the National

Basketball Association!" As a tall person, it is reassuring to be able to share an experience and confide in other tall people about the things that we go through. Tall people have to make adjustments all the time. We have to continually make sure that we do things differently so that we can fit in to a world that's not designed for us. Where do we find clothing? Where do you find shoes? Where do you finding nice clothing and shoes? Where do you find vehicles that work for us? How do you deal with tall person health problems? Where do you find chairs? What do you do when you get asked, "Do you play basketball?" so many times? How do you deal with being looked at in a different way? Having others around or within reach to connect to and having that support can make all the difference in a tall person's life. It helps us realize that I'm not going crazy.

The same thing applies to leadership. Having the opportunity to connect with other leaders in an educational association, social group, within your district, or an educational leader mastermind group can be life changing. It is a good leadership strategy to bounce ideas and to share your experiences, so you realize that you are not crazy. It's okay.

In an effort to provide school leaders with opportunities to connect with other leaders and not Stand Tall Mastermind Group is a way to utilize technology to connect school Stand Tall Leaders with other Stand Tall Leaders. It is an opportunity for leaders to connect once a week utilizing a Zoom video conference for one hour. Leaders sign up for a cohort of about 6–10 attendees. The first 5–10 minutes provide a quick mini-lesson on how to improve your educational leadership and then the following time everyone can talk about what it is they are working on, what are they doing, and how they can support and help each other.

How often do you get out of your box to go see another box so that you can bring those ideas into your box? #standtallstatement

The Stand Tall Mastermind comradery and understanding from other Stand Tall Leaders refuels you as a leader. You realize that, I'm not out here doing this alone – especially, when you are the only educational leader in the building. At times we get caught up into the culture of whatever your district has and you need to have those who have different types of viewpoints and understanding in order to make an impact in your school. Many times the community requires leaders to think outside the box, but how often do you get out of your box to go see another box so that you can bring those ideas into your box?

If you are interested in joining a Stand Tall Mastermind Group, visit https://www.standtallsteve.com/mastermind-group

8.4.3. Be Mentored by Someone Who Leads

Find someone to look up to. Someone that you can aspire to be like. Maybe there is someone out there that you can gather ideas and knowledge from. It might not be easy to find that person. Everyone has flaws, but having someone that you can connect with and you can emulate parts or all of their leadership can help center you and provide Influence for you to be motivated to be the best you can be.

If you don't have someone that you can connect to directly, there are tons of different resources that are available to find someone. There are associations, books, videos, different educators on social media that you can follow. Discover their path so that you can connect with and emulate what it is they are about and what it is that they are doing. You don't have to like everything they do. It may be just a part of who they are as a leader that you respect and look up to. If you are a part of a Mastermind Group or if you are a part of a network of educators, talk to them about what you are looking for.

As leaders, we get stuck in our offices. We get stuck in our building. We get stuck in our hallways. We get stuck in our classrooms. Sometimes we don't take the initiative to reach out and network, connect and find other people that will help strengthen us. Educational leaders' choices for professional development are not very vast. Most of the time you are required to give the professional development instead of attending the professional development.

Finding just one person you can look up to that will allow you to get that additional professional development that might not be in a book or a college course or podcast, ain't easy. Consider finding multiple individuals and sources for the different areas of leadership. Diversify! Not everyone person has everything that you need.

> Get an ego check! It doesn't matter if you have been an amazing leader for years. It doesn't matter if you have perfect outcomes. It doesn't matter if you think you are the smartest person in the school or district. You need to get out of your own way and look for a mentor. Everyone can use some improvement. Don't let the position get to your head. Eat a little humble pie.

Stand Tall Action

Find someone that you can mentor to help pull them along and share your knowledge and share what you have done well. Be vulnerable with them.

Find a network of people that are connected with you that you can share ideas, bounce things off of. It helps to know that you are not going crazy.

Find a mentor, someone that you can look up to. Mentors can be scares. You may need to diversify and pull the parts that you need from multiple people and locations. Having that well-rounded trifecta of leadership will allow you to be a much better stand tall leader.

Stand Tall Ideas

Restroom Signs

Organize a group of students who are artistic and positive. Work with the students on finding quotes and sayings that are inspiring to them and have conversations about whether these are appropriate and inspiring to others. In the ladies' room, you might use "You Look Great!" "You Can Do It!" or "Who Cares What They Say!" In the boys' room: "You Got This!" "You Da Man!" or "You Got Game!" Ask them to paint the quotes on the walls of the restrooms to completely change the environment. Use bright colors and bold letters so the messages can be seen. If you are unable to paint in the restrooms, make some signs and have them laminated. Be sure to use strong tape so they stay up.

Photo Op

Purchase a photo backdrop printed with the school logo on it – easily transportable types are available. Pull it out for special events so students, parents, and families can take photos in front of it. This is great for concerts – parents love to take photos of their children after concerts with their instrument. It is also great for recognition ceremonies. For a fun event activity, keep some props in a box so people can make funny faces and dress up, like a photo booth at a party.

8.5. Be a Finisher!

One of the most common realities within schools is that things tend to fizzle out and not finish. There are so many times that projects, programs, and concepts start in a school with gusto and excitement. Many times, people are on board and ready to make an impact on learning, culture, or relationships, but over time, the momentum fades, reality sets in and the last homestead holdouts stop caring. You hear statements like:

- "Are we still doing that. . .?"
- "What happened to that. . .?"
- "Remember when we did that. . .?"
- "Were we supposed to do something with that. . .?"

I truly believe that most ideas and programs that start within a school are valid and good. Educators are smart. Those who create programs and develop ideas are smart people. For the most part, they attended college, have a decent amount of sense to organize the program, and usually care enough to put the initial time in to make it work. The reason why programs are not successful and fade away is because of a lack of needed leadership and influence on those who are implementing and benefiting from the program or initiative. The need and desire for the leader to properly connect the outcomes of the program to the overall vision and dedicate to finishing it is lacking.

What does it mean to finish? Finishing is different, depending on the action and need. Finishing could be a confirmed date and time. Finishing could be measured outcomes connected to data. Finishing could be a feeling of completeness. Finishing could be a common understanding of accomplishment. Regardless of what being finished is, when do you know you have reached it? Do leaders have the tenacity, patience, and foresight to make it to the end? I would argue that many do not. In many cases, a leader starts with all intention of being successful and working through the motions to ensure that the program or actions are taking place. Although, throughout the process things happen. The leader at times becomes reactionary to the changes, loses sight of the vision, and then starts to blame others when things don't go as planned and eventually fades away. What can be done to change that?

A leader must do what is necessary to bring things to completion. Completion must be clearly outlined from the start and shared with others so they can see the vision. Having a clear sense of what completion looks like and feels like make a huge impact on the probability of success. The need and desire to complete a task needs to be put into the forefront of the new actions. Start with the intention to finish and finish well. That clearly stated intention is what will help influence others and strengthen the desire to make it to the end. Consider outlining with others what completion would look like and then what would completion would look like done well. Understanding the difference between the two strengthens your desire to complete the task. It presents the need for reflection and clarifies the standard of excellence or lack of excellence that is acceptable within your school.

A leader is doing this to move peoples' thinking from compliance to commitment. Finishing the project will put you into compliance. Completing the project well moves you into commitment.

8.5.1. Faith and Vision

What do you believe? Do you truly believe that it will get done? Look at who you are working with. What does your team look like? What is the level of efficiency vs. effectiveness within your team? What is the level of your influence? You have to believe that it can happen. At the onset of a project or program we tend to be overly optimistic. Does that optimism reflect your true beliefs? Do you have finishing faith? Just because you have the faith to start doesn't mean you have the faith to finish.

Faith is confidence or trust in a person or thing, or a belief not based on proof. You do not have the proof yet that this will finish. As a leader you need to have the confidence to know that it will finish. Showing that level of confidence will translate to those who follow you. That is the essence of influence. Yes, there will be those who are cynical and will push back against your confidence and Influence. Nevertheless, there are those who will attach their belief to the confidence and influence of the leader. Having that strong confidence regardless of not having the proof of success provides motivation and focus on making sure you finish well.

"Vision excites my future but frustrates my present." This quote is one of my favorites of all time. In order to be a leader who finishes well you must have vision. You must have a picture in your mind of what the end looks like. What is the big picture that you are operating from? A vision should get you excited about what is to come. The future is exciting because that is where the finish line is. The outcomes that are expected at that time will move the school forward in a direction that is purposeful and full of results. That picture of the future needs to be shared from you the Stand Tall Leader to those who are following you. Sharing that picture of the future finish line is what binds others together. The other side of this is that presently, you are not there yet. Your current situation may be light years away from that finish line vision. Looking around at what you currently have may be depressing and definitely frustrating. The goal is to take that frustration and turn it into motivation in order to make it to the end and finish what was started.

> **"Vision excites my future but frustrates my present."**
> **#standtallstatement**

8.5.2. Without Vision, You Have No Measure to Determine Progress

How else will you know that you are moving in the right direction unless you have a vision of where you want to be? Without vision your actions are not directed toward an outcome that is measurable. If others who are following you do not have the vision that you have for the future, they will be working from day to day with no true direction. The impact they will have on the students and school will be minimal. The conversations they will have with each other will be conflicting. How is this developing an environment of success? How can others know they are doing the right thing? How can anyone compare success with each other without it? Even if they are past compliance and are committed, without seeing your vision they are not *committed to what you truly respect and value.*

> **If others who are following you do not have the vision that you have for the future, they will be working from day to day with no true direction.**
> **#standtallstatement**

As much as we could argue about the need or validity of state and national testing, there is vision within those assessments. With every assessment given to students at the state level there has to be a vision of what the end game looks like. The vision may be the expected growth outcome, grade level mark, or overall mean score. Either way you look at it, there is a clear, expected outcome for those taking the assessment. It does not matter if we agree with it or not, it is there. It helps us to measure how well or how poorly we are doing. We can then ask ourselves, what else needs to be done to get back on track? The same is true related to leadership and finishing. Have a clear vision of what you want and make sure everyone knows. That way you can measure your success as you move closer to finishing.

Without vision, you have no measure to determine progress. #standtallstatement

Having vision, sharing vision, and finishing the vision is not easy for most people. There are several reasons why some leaders have difficulty with having vision and finishing.

8.5.3. Why You Would Have No Vision

- Too many mistakes
- On an island (nobody else is with you)
- Can't articulate

8.5.3.1. Too Many Mistakes

Okay, I get it! You have made a lot of mistakes. Because of those mistakes, you are skeptical of your abilities to get it done. You tend to second guess yourself a lot and maybe spin out of control, ultimately, not developing a clear vision and not finishing. Give me a break! Who hasn't made mistakes? I know that I have made more mistakes than is allowable per year. I'm probably making a mistake right now and I don't even realize it. The goal is to get over it. You can be your own worst critic. The goal is to get over the pity party, reflect on what you did wrong, fix it with integrity, and move on. There is nothing wrong with rewriting the narrative of the vision. If and when that happens, be sure to share why you did it and own it. As educators, we teach our students all the time to learn from the mistakes, but we don't always take our own advice. Multiple mistakes should not be a reason to prevent you from having vision. Did you ever think that the reason why you are making mistakes is because you don't have a vision?

8.5.3.2. On an Island

It's no secret that leadership is lonely. In many cases, you might be the only leader in your building or department. You may have other leaders around you, but you don't have the time to collaborate or share ideas in order to get affirmation that your vision is a good one. You are always thinking, ". . . is this right?" Basically, you are on an island by yourself trying to do this leadership thing. Your personal vision is just that – yours. You don't know if anyone else will accept it, understand it, or even care. Because you are on this island, you tend to second guess your decisions and vision. Therefore, the vision you have isn't shared or overdeveloped because it is now crowded on your island of one.

Hey! This is the job! You are in this position to make decisions and develop the vision. Yes, you will need others to support you and bounce things off of. It is up to you to make a raft, paddle off your island, go to another island, and share. With the multitude of ways to communicate and connect with other leaders, there is no reason why your vision cannot be shared and vetted with like-minded leaders. Being on an island regularly can tend to make leaders self-conscious about sharing and feel judged. After all, I've been riding solo for so long I don't know if I can take criticism pointing out my mistakes. Didn't you just read the above paragraphs about making mistakes and developing vision? Get over it!

8.5.3.3. Can't Articulate

Presentation is everything. I think back to *The Cosby Show* episode when his daughter's new boyfriend did not make a good impression on him and the family. Heathcliff explained to the boyfriend that the way he presented himself was like serving a beautiful steak dinner on a garbage can lid. The presentation ruined the dinner.

It is important to find a way to tell the story of the vision. Fine, you are not good at public speaking or storytelling. There are many other ways to articulate the vision and make it real for others.

- Write it down.
- Tell a personal story connected to the vision.
- Connect it to a moment in history.
- Make a rhyme.
- Use an image.
- Draw a picture.
- Challenge others to articulate it for you.

Vision is not a straight shot! It does not go directly from point A to point B. The goal is to remain aware of the vision. Keep the vision in the forefront of the activity or project. Roy Disney stated, "When the vision is clear, decisions are easy." Making decisions and actions within the oversight of your vision should become easier. The actions within those decisions may vary and have unexpected turns. New revelations may come about because of the actions being done. Understand that the actions to get to the vision will weave and move. Nevertheless, staying dedicated to the vision and finishing strong will result in positive outcomes.

8.5.4. To Be a Finisher

- *Have a squad.* Who is your crew? When you are ready to go out and hit the town, who do you call? You need people who've got your back and know what they don't know and are okay with that. The squad is for the middle of the process of working through the vision. Vision at the start is clear. Vision at the end is when you are celebrating. The squad in the middle will support you, push you, keep you focused, help do the work, continue to be progressive. The squad will push away distractions and things that do not fit within the vision. The squad will keep you humble and pump you up. As long as your squad can see the vision, you can be a Stand Tall Leader who finishes.
- *Be an abstract artist.* As an artist of abstract work, you have a basic vision of what the final product will be, but it's not exact. The process of creating the vision is the exciting part. As it is being created, it may not go exactly as planned but it's okay – that is the process of developing the vision. Let it go. Some paint may splatter to the side. A color may mix with another color unexpectedly. The brush stroke might cover an unexpected area. Let it go! Does the work of art convey the purpose of the vision? Is the work of art successful? Remember, it IS a work of art when it is finished!

Stay stubborn. My dog Mason is stubborn. He is a beagle, and beagles are known for being stubborn. The one thing he is most stubborn about is when he has picked up a scent that he MUST follow. It is in his DNA. There isn't much I can do to stop him from wanting to find what made that scent. Even though I yell at him and threaten him to come, he just can't let it go. I have to physically pull him away or pick him up in order to get him to move. Even after I do it, he is still thinking about it and wants to go back to finish. You need to be stubborn with your vision and your desire to finish. "I won't stop until the vision is fulfilled." Stay on it. Own it. You will continue working hard to make sure that it is complete. Don't let it go, keep it in the forefront. Brand it! Be a stubborn Stand Tall Leader.

ARE YOU A STAND TALL LEADER?

Being a Stand Tall Leader isn't as much about the specific actions you do, but more about a way of thinking and belief system, then manifesting that belief into your leadership. Being a Stand Tall Leader is about being purposeful with your thoughts and actions within your leadership.

My mantra for life is, "When you stand TALL, you don't think small." Hopefully, now that you have read Stand Tall Leadership, you have a deeper understanding of how that statement can mean so much to you. Now that you know what you know about being a Stand Tall Leader, you have a new perspective of your life as a leader. You have a new awareness of your school or district and your role within it. Now that you know what you know, you can't think smaller. Your vision is bigger. Your vision is wider. Now that you know what you know, and you can do what you do, how in the world can you think less? How can you do less? You cannot think like a small leader. You are TALL! You are larger than life.

Because You Are a Stand Tall Leader

- You can see that what you *respect and value* develops your level of *influence* that connects to your *integrity* that allows others to move from *compliance to commitment.*
- You are able to make *decisions* that are specific to the situation at hand and connects with the *scheduled culture* so that it can temper the *climate.*
- You can see that the *climate changes* from day to day and you can use your *influence* to alter the *behavioral culture* so that the climate remains more *consistent* around what you *respect* and *value.*
- You can speak to *parents on the phone* with confidence so that what is said moves the conversation toward agreement.
- You can identify *who you can help* and *who you can't help* so that you are not wasting your time an energy and therefore able to balance the level of *efficiency and effectiveness* of your work.

- You understand that *administrator guilt* is real, and it is okay for you to take the time to *reflect* on your practice so that you can continue to be the best Stand Tall Leader.
- You now will expand your *influence by mentoring* others to become Stand Tall Leaders while you seek out other Stand Tall Leaders in order to support each other and continue to grow by putting your ego in check and be *mentored* by someone.
- You will be a *finisher* so that your *vision* will become reality.

Close your eyes and imagine if you implemented everything you now know about being a Stand Tall Leader. Imagine the level of influence you could have. Imagine the outcomes you would see. Imagine the culture and climate you would develop.

Close your eyes again. Now imagine if you did nothing. Imagine if you knew all that you now know, and you did nothing. Imagine the level of influence you would have. Imagine the outcomes you would get. Imagine the culture and climate you would develop.

Don't take that chance. Step it up! Implement what you now know into your leadership and be the Stand Tall Leader you know you can be. When you stand TALL, you don't think small.

ABOUT THE AUTHOR

Steve Bollar, a.k.a. Stand Tall Steve, is driven to help schools, associations, and organizations create a better culture and climate through common sense, personal experiences and encouragement. His book *Ideas, Ideas, Ideas!* has been a jumping point for hundreds of organizations on how to increase the morale, change the culture, and strengthen the climate for their students and staff.

In 2014, Steve was awarded the Burlington County Principals and Supervisors Association Visionary Leadership Award. In 2011, Steve was recognized by *South Jersey Magazine* as one of South Jersey's Top 20 Men of the Year. Additionally, Steve was chosen by *Suburban Family* magazine Top 20 Citizen of the Year for 2012. Steve is also a member of the Jostens Renaissance Hall of Fame. Renaissance is a program that focuses on recognizing students and staff while developing a positive school culture.

Steve served on the board of directors of the New Jersey Principals and Supervisors Association. NJPSA is the premier supporting organization for New Jersey principals and supervisors.

Steve has a long history in the education system, from art teacher to principal to superintendent of schools. His 25+-year career has shown him firsthand how to face the challenges that any organization can encounter and how to overcome them with creativity and communication.

It's this insight that he brings to the stage during his keynotes, breakouts, and workshops – training administration, teachers, organizations, and staff on how to create a better atmosphere for students and staff alike.

INDEX